to

Build Faith

Suzanne Bower

Introduction:

The statement "The just shall live by faith" is repeated four times in the Bible. (Habakkuk 2:4, Romans 1:17, Galatians 3:11, Hebrews 10:38)

This being the case, it seems it would be to our advantage to understand what faith is!

This book is comprised of meditations, which are designed to build confidence in a loving Heavenly Father who desires only good for his children, and the power of faith in God's Word to execute His promises to His children.

Contents:

What is Faith ?

When the disciples asked Jesus "Lord, teach us to pray", Jesus answered them by saying:

Our Father which art in heaven, Hallowed be thy name. Thy kingdom come. Thy will be done in earth, as it is in heaven. (Matthew 6:10)

Notice He told them to ask that it be in earth as it is in Heaven.   This is a powerful statement. Faith is the hand that reaches into Heaven and brings Heaven to earth.

Furthermore, Jesus says "<u>Thy will be done</u> on earth as it is in Heaven." We can infer from this that it is God's will that earth be like Heaven. This passage illustrates this concept further:

Therefore shall ye lay up these my words in your heart and in your soul, and bind them for a sign upon your hand, that they may be as frontlets between your eyes.

And ye shall teach them your children, speaking of them when thou sittest in thine house, and

7

when thou walkest by the way, when thou liest down, and when thou risest up.

And thou shalt write them upon the door posts of thine house, and upon thy gates:

That your days may be multiplied, and the days of your children, in the land which the LORD sware unto your fathers to give them, as the days of heaven upon the earth.
(Deuteronomy 11:18 - 21)

Notice God is commanding them to "lay up" His Word in their hearts so that their days would be as "days of heaven upon the earth".

Why is it necessary to "lay up", or store, the Word in our hearts? We see in this passage that faith comes by hearing the Word of God.

So then faith cometh by hearing and hearing by the Word of God. (Romans 10:17)

We see that hearing the Word of God builds faith. So we are to study the Word in order to build faith. Why, then, is faith so important?

We see that the statement "The just shall live by faith" is repeated four times in the Bible. (Habakkuk 2:4, Romans 1:17, Galatians 3:11, Hebrews 10:38) This being the case, it seems it would be to our advantage to understand what faith is!

The Bible states further "Whatever is not of faith is sin". (Romans 14:23)   This is much stronger still.

The Greek word *pistis* translated as faith, means "trust" or "moral conviction of religious truth".

The writer of the book of Hebrews says "Faith is the substance of things hoped for, the evidence of things not seen" (Hebrews 11:1)

Let's "unpack" this.

The word translated as "substance" can also be translated as "assurance".   And the word translated as "evidence" can also be translated as "proof".   So we can paraphrase this verse by saying "Faith is the assurance of things hoped for, the proof of things unseen".

This is very powerful.   The PROOF of things unseen.

What it comes down to is that when faith is present, and you pray in faith, you have the confidence that what you are believing will come to pass.

This is what Jesus is saying here:

And Jesus answering saith unto them, Have faith in God.

For verily I say unto you, That whosoever shall say unto this mountain, Be thou removed, and be thou cast into the sea; and shall not doubt in his heart, but shall believe that those things which he saith shall come to pass; he shall have whatsoever he saith. (Mark 11:23)

I am sure you are asking "How does one get this kind of faith?" (!)

The Bible tells us we do it this way.

Faith comes by hearing, and hearing by the Word of God. (Romans 10:17)

So, then, faith comes by hearing the Word of God. We build our faith by reading God's Word and meditating on it.

This book of the law shall not depart out of thy mouth; but thou shalt meditate therein day and night, that thou mayest observe to do according to all that is written therein: for then thou shalt make thy way prosperous, and then thou shalt have good success. (Joshua 1:8)

We see that "meditating" on God's Word continually will cause us to "prosper" and have "good success". The Hebrew word translated as "meditate" means "to mutter softly to oneself". In so doing, we are allowing ourself to hear the Word and build our faith in the Word, so that when we speak the Word into our lives we do so "without doubting in our heart" and believing that the things we say shall "come to pass". Then according to Jesus they SHALL come to pass.

Faith is the hand that reaches into Heaven and brings "Heaven to earth".

The following chapters are a collection of articles which were written to help build faith. At the end of the book are a collection of Scriptures on which to meditate to build faith for particular circumstances and speak in prayer in faith believing to receive what God has told is already done.

My prayer is that anyone reading this book will master the art of living by faith on the highest level and walking with Jesus to see His plan of Heaven on Earth come to pass in their lives and the lives of all they touch.

Believe the Love

And we have known and believed the love that God hath to us. God is love; and he that dwelleth in love dwelleth in God, and God in him.
(1John 4:16)

This Scripture contains a powerful message. "And we have known and believed the love that God has toward us".

How many of us truly believe that God loves us?

It is essential to comprehend the love of God toward us in order to receive all that God has provided for us through Jesus. If we do not truly believe God loves us, then we cannot believe that He has provided "all things that pertain to life and godliness". (2 Peter 1:3)

Most Christians are familiar with the following commandments of Jesus:

And thou shalt love the Lord thy God with all thy heart, and with all thy soul, and with all thy mind, and with all thy strength: this is the first commandment.

And the second is like, namely this, Thou shalt love thy neighbour as thyself. There is none other commandment greater than these.
(Mark 12:30, 31)

And we usually strive to "love our neighbors as ourselves". But this is getting the "cart before the horse", as they say.

Notice the first commandment Jesus gives is to "love the Lord thy God, will all they heart, soul, mind and strength".

But how does one do this?

I believe that this scripture answers that question:

And hope maketh not ashamed; because the love of God is shed abroad in our hearts by the Holy Ghost which is given unto us. Romans 5:5

It is the love of God, or God's love, that is "shed abroad in our hearts".

In order to "love our neighbor as ourselves", we must first receive the love of God, or, in other words, we must believe the love God has for us.

In order to comprehend the love God has for us we need to meditate on the Scriptures which speak of His love for us.

14

Let us examine some of them.

But God commendeth his love toward us, in that, while we were yet sinners, Christ died for us. (Romans 5:8)

Notice, "while we were yet sinners", God sent His son to die for us. We did nothing to deserve it, but God had a plan to redeem us and bless us.

But there is more. Jesus prayed this prayer as He was waiting in the Garden to go to the cross:

And the glory which thou gavest me I have given them; that they may be one, even as we are one:

I in them, and thou in me, that they may be made perfect in one; and that the world may know that thou hast sent me, and hast loved them, as thou hast loved me. (John 17:22, 23)

Notice, Jesus is saying that God has loved us as He loves Jesus. This is difficult to fathom. God loves us with the same love that He loves Jesus. We need to meditate on this until it becomes a reality in our hearts.

The power to fulfil the Word is contained in the Word itself.

The literal translation of Luke 1:37 is "No Word of God is without power".

As we meditate on these Scriptures pertaining to the Love of God toward us until it manifests in our hearts, then it will flow freely from God to us, and through us to others.

We cannot manufacture this kind of love by simply deciding to love others. This kind of love is a spiritual force that flows from the heart of God to us and through us and is available to us through His Word.

"In the beginning was the Word, and the Word was with God, and the Word was God".
(John 1:1)

As we meditate on God's Word, we "behold" Him, and as we behold Him we are changed into His image.

But we all, with open face beholding as in a glass the glory of the Lord, are changed into the same image from glory to glory, even as by the Spirit of the Lord. (2 Corinthians 3:18)

And further:

God is love (I John 4:8)

So as we behold God's love in His Word, and in His Presence in worship, we are changed into His image of love, and then His love will flow freely through us to others.

The Name of Jesus

The name "Jesus" is a transliteration of the Hebrew name *"Yeshua"* which means literally "God saves".

Jesus Himself told us,

And whatsoever ye shall ask <u>in my name</u>, that will I do, that the Father may be glorified in the Son. If ye shall ask any thing <u>in my name</u>, I will do it. (John 14:13,14)

Hitherto have ye asked nothing <u>in my name</u>: ask, and ye shall receive, that your joy may be full. (John 16, 24)

Here we have Jesus' own Word for it, whatever we ask the Father in His Name He will do.

But why is that? What is so special about praying in Jesus' Name?

Jesus said,

All power is given unto me in heaven and in earth. Go ye therefore... (Matthew 28:18)

17

The Greek word *ex-oo-see'-ah* translated here as "power" literally means "authority". So He is saying that all authority in Heaven and earth has been given to Him, therefore **we** are to go… Go and do what? We see this same event recorded in the Gospel of Mark this way.

Go ye into all the world, and preach the gospel to every creature…
And these signs shall follow them that believe; In my name shall they cast out devils; they shall speak with new tongues; They shall take up serpents; and if they drink any deadly thing, it shall not hurt them; they shall lay hands on the sick, and they shall recover. (Mark 16:16-18)

There it is again "in My Name". And what are we to do? Go into all the world and preach the gospel to every creature. And the signs shall follow those that believe in the Name of Jesus are that they will have supernatural power over evil spirits, they shall have supernatural languages, supernatural protection, and supernatural power to heal the sick. These are all things that Jesus did, and now He is commanding believers to do likewise.

What is being described here is a transfer of authority. It is the same type of transfer of authority that takes place when a person is given "power of attorney". In this case a person is given the legal right to perform legal transactions in another person's name. Essentially what is happening here is that Jesus is giving those who believe on His name the power of attorney, or the legal right to use His name on this earth. This is the reason the part of the Bible written after His death is referred to as the New "Testament". A testament declares the will of the testator, or the one who writes it, which is to come into effect after the testator dies. Jesus was given "all power in Heaven and earth" and when He left the earth he delegated that authority to us, the believers. But, in order to exercise it we must use His Name, because He is the one to whom it was actually given. We have the authority to use His Name. And, at that Name, every knee in Heaven and earth and under the earth has to bow.

Wherefore God also hath highly exalted him [Jesus], *and given him a name which is above every name: That at the name of Jesus every knee should bow, of things in heaven, and things in earth, and things under the earth.* (Philippians 2:9, 10)

Sickness has a name. But, the Name of Jesus is higher. Poverty has a name. But, the Name of Jesus is higher. Failure has a name. Fear has a name. But, Praise God! the name of Jesus is higher. All these things have to bow at the Name of Jesus.

We have authority to use His name by virtue of the new birth. When we receive Christ by faith and are born again into the Kingdom of God, we are now *in* Christ (2 Corinthians 1:21), and therefore have the legal right to use His Name.

In the book of Acts, we read about a man who had been lame from birth. He was waiting outside the gate (which was called "Beautiful") of the temple. When he saw Peter and Paul he was about to ask them for alms (money) but Peter said to him,

Silver and gold have I none; but such as I have give I thee: <u>In the name of Jesus Christ </u>of Nazareth rise up and walk. And he took him by the right hand, and lifted him up: and immediately his feet and ankle bones received strength.

And he leaping up stood, and walked, and entered with them into the temple, walking, and leaping, and praising God. (Acts 3:6-8)

When Peter commanded him to walk "in the Name of Jesus", immediately he received strength to walk. And all the people who were used to seeing the lame man every day before the temple came to Peter and Paul "greatly wondering". Peter asked them "Why do you marvel at this?" and he began to tell them that Jesus, whom they had delivered up to Pontius Pilate and desired to be crucified, God had raised from the dead. He went on to say,

And his name through faith in his name hath made this man strong, whom ye see and know... (Acts 3:16)

It was faith "in the Name of Jesus" which made the man strong.

The following day the rulers and elders and the high priest had Peter and Paul brought before them and asked them,

By what power, or by what name, have ye done this? (Acts 4:7)

Notice the rulers asked "by what name" did you do this? And Peter and Paul answered,

B*e it known unto you all, and to all the people of Israel, that by the name of Jesus Christ of Nazareth, whom ye crucified, whom God raised from the dead, even by him doth this man stand here before you whole.* (Acts 4:10)

Again, they took no credit to themselves, but proclaim that it was "by the Name of Jesus Christ" that the man was made whole.

Notice the result of this,

But that it spread no further among the people, let us straitly threaten them, that they speak henceforth to no man in this name. (Acts 4:17)

The rulers forbid them to speak "in this name", the Name of Jesus. They did not forbid Peter and Paul to speak at all, only in the name of Jesus.

So we see that the authority is in the Name of Jesus, not in Peter or Paul for who they were, but in the Name of Jesus, <u>whose</u> they were. Which is why, since we have been born again and He lives in us (John 14:23), and He has made us one with Himself and the Father (John 17:23), we also have that same authority in His Name.

Therefore, as the apostle Paul admonishes us,

And whatsoever ye do in word or deed, <u>do all in the name of the Lord Jesus</u>, giving thanks to God and the Father by him. (Colossians 3:17)

God Gave His Word

Wherein God, willing more abundantly to shew unto the heirs of promise the immutability of his counsel, confirmed it by an oath:
That by two immutable things, in which it was impossible for God to lie,... (Hebrews 6:17, 18)

Often, when I am praying, the Lord will "speak" to me. It is not an audible voice, it is just a thought, which comes to mind, and I know it is the Lord, as I know His Presence, and I know His Peace that accompanies the thought. There is often the reminder of a Scripture, which confirms it, or the chapter and verse to look up to confirm it.

One day when I was praying about a certain problem and struggling somewhat to get into faith to believe God's promise for it, the Lord said to me, "I have given you my Word".

This made a tremendous impact on me. I seriously had never considered God's Word in this light before.

We have most of us heard the saying "Your word is your bond".

23

At one time, a legal agreement was entered into merely by both parties agreeing, in other words, "giving their word", and shaking hands. No attorneys, contracts, or other legal procedure was necessary. A man's word was his "bond" and was considered as such.

Notice what the above Scripture reference is saying. God wanted to "show" (demonstrate) to the "heirs of promise" (that's us!) the "immutability of His counsel", in other words the unchangeableness, or the trustworthiness, of His Word. What this means is that when God gives His Word, He keeps it.

Notice the second verse says it is impossible for God to lie.

So when God has said:

I am the Lord that healeth thee. (Exodus 15:26)

And the LORD will take away from thee all sickness, (Deuteronomy 7:15)

and further,
Himself bore our sickness and our diseases
(Matthew 8:17)

...and by His stripes you were healed.
(I Peter 2:24)

we can say with confidence "Father, you have given your Word that Jesus bore my sickness and my diseases and by His stripes I was healed, so I receive that healing now, and from this moment on I will just thank Him and praise you until I see it manifest".

When we see:

My God shall supply all your need according to His riches in glory by Christ Jesus (Philippians 4:19)

and we have a bill we don't know how to pay, we can say with confidence "Father, you have given me your Word that you will supply all my need according to your riches in glory by Christ Jesus, so I receive your provision now and know I can count on you to provide. From this time on I will just thank you and praise you that it is already done and obey whatever you lead me to do".

When we find;

Casting your care upon Him for He careth for you. (I Peter 5:7),

we know that whatever concerns us for which we do not yet have a solution, we can trust Him to already have the answer and we can rest in Him with the confidence that He already has it worked out. We can say, "Lord, I cast the care of this situation onto you. I will not worry and fret over it, I will just trust you to show me the answer and work it out. You already know the solution and I just trust you to make it plain to me. I will just thank you and praise you until I see the answer."

When we see that Jesus said;

Verily, verily, I say unto you, Whatsoever ye shall ask the Father in my name, he will give it you.
Hitherto have ye asked nothing in my name: ask, and ye shall receive, that your joy may be full.
(John 16:23, 24)

we can have the confidence that whatever we ask the Father in Jesus' Name will be done according to Jesus' Word because He is faithful and He keeps His Word. This pretty much covers it all!

We have yet to fully grasp the power of God's Word.

When God speaks, the power of the Word He speaks causes it to manifest. When God said, "Light be", light came into being. (Genesis 1:3)

The Hebrew word *daw-bawr'*, translated as "word", is also translated as "thing" or "matter". In other words, the word is the thing it speaks of. They are inseparable.

26

The literal translation of Luke 1:37 from the original Greek text is; "No word of God is without power". In other words, the Word of God contains in itself the power to perform it.

For as the rain cometh down, and the snow from heaven, and returneth not thither, but watereth the earth, and maketh it bring forth and bud, that it may give seed to the sower, and bread to the eater:
So shall my word be that goeth forth out of my mouth: it shall not return unto me void, but it shall accomplish that which I please, and it shall prosper in the thing whereto I sent it.
(Isaiah 55:10,11)

Notice in this passage God is saying His Word will "prosper in the thing it was sent to do". In other words, the Word will perform what it was sent for. The power to perform the Word is in the Word itself.

Jesus said to the Father,

Thy Word is truth. (John 17:17)

He also said,

The words that I speak unto you, they are spirit, and they are life. (John 6:63)
The apostle John said:

In the beginning was the Word, and the Word was with God, and the Word was God..
(John 1:1)

So God is inseparable from His Word.

He said, further,

The Word became flesh and dwelt among us.
(John 1:14).

So, Jesus and the Word are one.

Consider the following passage of Scripture:

God... Hath in these last days spoken unto us by his Son, whom he hath appointed heir of all things, by whom also he made the worlds;
Who being the brightness of his glory, and the express image of his person, and upholding all things by the word of his power,...
(Hebrews 1:1-3)

We see by the above passage that God, by Jesus, (Who is the Word "made flesh") made the world, and is upholding all things by "the word of His power". In other words, the power of God, contained in His Word, is what is holding the world together!

When we get the revelation of the power and the truth of God's Word, we will not have to struggle to believe. Faith will become a way of life so that we will "live by faith".

The just shall live by faith" (Habakkuk 2:4, Romans 1:17, Galatians 3:11, Hebrews 10:38)

Recall what Jesus said:

Therefore I say unto you, What things soever ye desire, when ye pray, believe that ye receive them, and ye shall have them. (Mark 11:24)

Notice, He said "When you pray, believe you receive ", not "When you see it, believe you receive".

He gave His Word. Believe it!

Intimacy With the Father

Jesus said:

God is a Spirit: and they that worship him must worship him in spirit and in truth. (John 4:24)

It seems very few Christians actually understand the concept of worship, and yet, this is the most fundamental concept of our relationship with God. Worship is coming into a place of intimacy with God where all we see is Him and nothing matters except being in His presence and experiencing His love, His joy, His peace and the knowledge of Him.

In the Old Testament, marriage is used as an example of God's relationship with Israel.

Not according to the covenant that I made with their fathers in the day that I took them by the hand to bring them out of the land of Egypt; which my covenant they brake, although I was an husband unto them, saith the LORD: (Jeremiah 31:32)

In the New Testament, the Church is referred to as the "Bride of Christ". (II Cor 11:2, Rev 22:17)

In a marriage relationship there is a God-given way of attaining intimacy which is unique to that relationship. It involves total concentration on the object of love. Worship is a total concentration on the Father, with nothing else distracting attention.

Many times we unwillingly substitute service for worship. We see an example of this in this passage:

Now it came to pass, as they went, that he entered into a certain village: and a certain woman named Martha received him into her house.
And she had a sister called Mary, which also sat at Jesus' feet, and heard his word.
But Martha was cumbered about much serving, and came to him, and said, Lord, dost thou not care that my sister hath left me to serve alone? bid her therefore that she help me.
And Jesus answered and said unto her, 'Martha, Martha, thou art careful and troubled about many things:
But one thing is needful: and Mary hath chosen that good part, which shall not be taken away from her.' (Luke 10:38 - 42)

Mary has chosen the "one thing" that is needful, to sit at the feet of Jesus and learn from Him.

As if that were not clear enough, Jesus also said:

If ye abide in me, and my words abide in you, ye shall ask what ye will, and it shall be done unto you. (John 15:7)

In this place of intimacy with the Father through the Son, is everything we need.

Some years ago I was going through a very difficult time and when I prayed the Lord only said "Get up early and praise me". This was very difficult to do as I was not a morning person! So finally I remembered to ask Him to enable me to do this. I don't know why it took so long to ask as I am thoroughly familiar with the fact that "Without me [Jesus] you can do nothing" (John 15:5)

At first, it was all I could do to get up 15 minutes early and pray. I had difficulty concentrating this early in the morning, but discovered once I began to do this everything changed. As I spent time before the Lord, with no distractions, I was able to "tune in" to Him and hear His voice and sense His leading. Everything began to change. My attitude toward the people around me changed, and their attitude toward me changed. His Presence began to permeate my day and everything I did. My relationship with Him was no longer an occasional visit, but a continual fellowship. Answers to prayer began to come in awesome and amazing ways. Now I set my alarm at least an hour early every day to make

sure that I do not neglect this precious time with
Him.

*... and truly our fellowship is with the Father,
and with his Son Jesus Christ.* (1John 1:3)

And again, we can say with the apostle Paul:

*For in him we live, and move, and have our
being; as certain also of your own poets have
said, For we are also his offspring.* (Acts 17:28)

From this place of rest and peace springs
everything we need, protection, provision,
healing, strength and power.

*He that dwelleth in the secret place of the most
High shall abide under the shadow of the
Almighty.
I will say of the LORD, He is my refuge and my
fortress: my God; in him will I trust.
Because he hath set his love upon me, therefore
will I deliver him: I will set him on high, because
he hath known my name.
He shall call upon me, and I will answer him: I
will be with him in trouble; I will deliver him,
and honour him.
With long life will I satisfy him, and shew him my
salvation.* (Psalms 91:2, 14, 15, 16)

And here we see:

Thou wilt keep him in perfect peace, whose mind is stayed on thee: because he trusteth in thee. (Isaiah 26:3)

The Hebrew word *shalom* translated as "peace" means "safety, health, prosperity, peace: nothing broken, nothing missing." And He will keep us in **perfect peace** if we keep our mind on Him.

What a powerful promise!

And even more:

Thou wilt shew me the path of life: in thy presence is fulness of joy; at thy right hand there are pleasures for evermore. (Psalm 16:11)

In His Presence is fullness of joy. You can't have any more joy than that.

Last, and most important:

But we all, with open face beholding as in a glass the glory of the Lord, are changed into the same image from glory to glory, even as by the Spirit of the Lord. (II Corinthians 3:18)

What we behold is what we become. As we spend time in His presence beholding Him, we are "changed into his image from glory to glory". It just doesn't get any better than this!

My prayer is that anyone reading this article will be drawn to a more intimate fellowship with the Father and His Son, Jesus Christ. Nothing this world has to offer can come close to comparing to this.

Know Your Enemy

One thing Christians need to know is that we have only one enemy, and that is the devil. People are not your enemies. The Bible tells us:

For we wrestle not against flesh and blood, but against principalities, against powers, against the rulers of the darkness of this world, against spiritual wickedness in high places.
(Ephesians 6:12)

Our real enemies are demonic forces, or agents of the devil.

People who do not know Christ really do not know why they do what they do. You are either being led by the Spirit of God, or you are controlled by the devil. The idea that you can be independent and in control of your life is the same lie that the devil told Adam and Eve in the garden. He said "You will be like gods", in other words, masters of your own destiny. The truth was, they became subject to his lies and victims of the curse.

We are free to choose, but the choice is either to be directed by God, in His divine wisdom and love, and follow the path he has prepared to bless us and give us abundance and peace, or to follow the devil and be victimized by the curse. There is nothing in between, and eventually we will pay the price of walking out of God's blessing.

Those who do not know, and have never known God and His wisdom, are bound by the lies of the devil that they do not have the wisdom to discern.

The good news is that we have been given authority over ALL the power of the enemy. Jesus said:

Behold, I give unto you power to tread on serpents and scorpions, and over all the power of the enemy (Luke10:19)

He also said:

Love your enemies, bless them that curse you, do good to them that hate you, and pray for them which despitefully use you, and persecute you; (Matthew 5:44)

These are not just platitudes and pleasant thoughts to take your mind off ugly behavior, this is an instruction to take your legal authority in Jesus' Name and set these people free from the lies of the devil that have held them in anger, unforgiveness, hatred and bitterness, which manifests in selfish, hurtful behavior.

The apostle Paul said:

For the weapons of our warfare are not carnal, but mighty through God to the pulling down of strong holds; Casting down imaginations, and every high thing that exalteth itself against the knowledge of God, and bringing into captivity every thought to the obedience of Christ;
(2 Corinthians 10:4, 5)

When we use the authority that Jesus has given us in His Name to declare liberty to the captives (Isaiah 61:1), pray the Father give them the spirit of wisdom and revelation in the knowledge of him, that the eyes of their understanding be enlightened that they may know the love of Christ and the power of His resurrection (Ephesians 1:17-19), eventually they will come.

One Thing is Needful

The just shall live by faith. (Habakkuk 2:4, Romans 1:17, Galatians 3:11, Hebrews 10:38)

We see it written four times that "The just shall live by faith". We know that if we are in Christ, we are "justified" by faith, (Galatians 2:26) so we are the "just". Therefore we need to know how to get this faith by which we must live.

We all (or at least most of us) have heard stories about people who have suddenly had faith to believe for a miracle in a time of crisis and have received their miracle. We also know of others in a similar crisis, who know the Lord and who trust Him, but nevertheless, have not received their miracle.

The reason is that there are two kinds of faith. The kind mentioned here is the kind spoken of in this passage:

But the manifestation of the Spirit is given to every man to profit withal.
For to one is given by the Spirit the word of wisdom; to another the word of knowledge by the same Spirit;

41

*To another **faith** by the same Spirit; to another the gifts of healing by the same Spirit;* (1 Corinthians 12:7- 9)

This kind of faith is given sovereignly by the Holy Spirit at His will and we cannot predict when or to whom this may happen. It is wonderful when it does, but it doesn't always occur.

Happily for us, there is another kind of faith that is available to every believer and it is received at the time of the new birth. This is the kind of faith which this passage discusses:

For I say, through the grace given unto me, to every man that is among you, not to think of himself more highly than he ought to think; but to think soberly, according as God hath dealt to every man the measure of faith. (Romans 12:3)

To appropriate this kind of faith and learn to use it, we must nurture it by feeding it on the Word.

The Bible talks of it as "exceedingly growing faith". (2 Thessalonians 1:3) And the way to "grow" it is with the Word.

So then faith cometh by hearing, and hearing by the word of God. (Romans 10:17)

I can personally testify that this kind of faith is available to anyone who will press in and receive it.

Jesus speaks of it here:

If you abide in me, and my words abide in you, you shall ask what you will, and it shall be done unto you. (John 15:7)

Here is an example of how this works. At one time I had lost the "umpteenth" job due to "absenteeism" from chronic sinus infection which had become resistant to antibiotics. In other words there was no "cure". I seemed to be doomed to being incapacitated every several months for two weeks or so, and employers frown on that. So I was diligently seeking God and praying and studying the Word when I found this passage and it came alive to me:

For verily I say unto you, That whosoever shall say unto this mountain, Be thou removed, and be thou cast into the sea; and shall not doubt in his heart, but shall believe that those things which he says shall come to pass; he shall have whatsoever he says.

Therefore I say unto you, Whatsoever things you desire, when you pray, believe that you receive them, and you shall have them. (Mark 11:22 -24)

Suddenly I saw it. "Whosoever" (this would be me) would have "whatsoever" they say, if they believe in their heart and do not doubt. And further "When you pray" believe you receive, not when you see it manifest, but *when you pray*, believe it is already yours. So I commanded the sinuses to drain and heal in Jesus name, without doubting, totally convinced it was done, and that was the end of the chronic sinusitis. (!) God is faithful.

From then on I was fixed. From that time until now, I continually strive to "abide in Jesus" and allow His Word to "abide in me" by spending enough time in the Word every day and in His presence, so that I can hear His voice when He speaks to me. Now understand, this is not an audible voice (although some may experience it that way) it is just a thought that comes to me that I know is Him, because I spend so much time in His presence I recognize it, and I spend enough time in His written Word that I can judge if what I am hearing lines up with His Word. If it is from God, it will never contradict His written Word.

So now I have the confidence that there is no problem that can surface in my life that He will not make a way, because He has promised "I will be with you in trouble and I will deliver you" (Psalm 91) and "He watches over His Word to perform it". (Jeremiah 1:12)

Another difference between this kind of faith and the first kind mentioned is that if the devil comes back with the same symptoms and tries to put the same condition on you again, you can run him off the next time just as you did the first time. And be assured, all sickness is a work of the devil as a result of the curse. There was no sickness in the Garden of Eden.

Recall the story of Mary and Martha, the sisters of Lazarus whom Jesus raised from the dead. When Jesus came to visit, Martha was busy getting the meal prepared and fussing around and complaining that Mary wouldn't help, and all Mary wanted to do was sit at the feet of Jesus and hear His Word. (Luke 10:39) Then Jesus said to Martha;

Martha, Martha, you are careful and troubled about many things:
But one thing is needful: and Mary has chosen that good part, which shall not be taken away from her. (Luke 10:42)

"One thing is needful"; and Mary had chosen that one thing. That "one thing" was to spend time with Jesus and hear His Words.

We have the Words of Jesus faithfully recorded in the gospels, and through the Holy Spirit in all the Scripture.

All scripture is given by inspiration of God, and is profitable for doctrine, for reproof, for correction, for instruction in righteousness: That the man of God may be perfect, thoroughly furnished unto all good works. (2Timothy 3:17)

This is the "one thing" that will suffice us, if we give it first priority. It we diligently "attend to God's Word" (Proverbs 4:20) it will build our faith to the point where we will be able to speak His Word concerning any situation and God's Word "will not return void, but will accomplish what it was sent forth to do" (Isaiah 55:11)

Remember *"No Word of God is without power"* (Luke 1:37 Greek New Testament)

And again, we have Jesus' Word on it that;

If you abide in me, and my words abide in you, you shall ask what you will, and it shall be done unto you. (John 15:7)

Quit Limiting God!

Someone may ask, "Can anyone limit God?"

Read what King David wrote:

Yea, they turned back and tempted God, and limited the Holy One of Israel. (Psalms 78:41)

We see that the "children" of Israel limited God. How did they limit Him?

Notice what the apostle Matthew said regarding Jesus:

...and he did not many mighty works there because of their unbelief. (Matthew 13:58)

So it is unbelief that limits God. This makes sense, as it is faith, or believing God, which releases His power in our lives, so by unbelief, which is the opposite of faith, we limit Him.

We need to get a revelation of the limitless, unbounded, eternal and infinite goodness of God.

47

We cannot really receive all that He has for us until we grasp Who He is and what He has already prepared for us "before the foundation of the world" (Ephesians 1:4) and this revelation can only come by "renewing our minds" in His Word (Romans 12:2)

But as it is written, Eye hath not seen, nor ear heard, neither have entered into the heart of man, the things which God hath prepared for them that love him.
But God hath revealed them unto us by his Spirit: for the Spirit searcheth all things, yea, the deep things of God. (1Corinthians 2:9, 10)

There is simply no substitute for "feeding" on the Word. Nothing else can transform our lives and bring us into the knowledge and understanding of our Heavenly Father as reading the Scriptures, which were given by God through the Holy Spirit and handed down from generation to generation since the beginning of human history, and by spending time in His Presence until we know His voice and can hear directly from Heaven, so that His Spirit can reveal to us His desires and plans for us. This is the only way to develop the faith to receive all He has prepared for us in His infinite love and mercy, since "before the foundation of the world"..

The apostle Paul tells us "Faith comes by hearing, and hearing by the Word of God". (Romans 10:17)

The Greek word translated as "word" here is *rhema*, which means "spoken word". So we need to hear the Word spoken.

Notice what the Lord told Joshua:

This book of the law shall not depart out of thy mouth; but thou shalt meditate therein day and night, that thou mayest observe to do according to all that is written therein: for then thou shalt make thy way prosperous, and then thou shalt have good success. (Joshua 1:8)

Notice: "shall not depart out of thy mouth". The Hebrew word translated as "meditate", means "to mutter" or to say softly, repeatedly.

When we read the Word and "meditate" on it, or say it to ourselves, over and over, we are "feeding" our "heart", or our spirit, on the Word and it eventually will become more real to us than our circumstances. Then we are saying it in faith and it will begin to manifest in our lives.

This is the way to receive healing, provision, deliverance, salvation for our families, or any other good thing that God has prepared for us.

It is through reading the Word, and seeing the promises that God has given, that we come to understand His will for us, so that we can ask in faith, believing and knowing, that what He has promised He will perform.

For example, meditating on the promises concerning healing builds faith for healing:

Himself [Jesus] *took our infirmities, and bare our sicknesses.* Matthew 8:17
   ...by whose stripes ye were healed.
(1 Peter 2:24)

Bless the LORD, O my soul, and forget not all his benefits:
*... who healeth **all** thy diseases;*
(Psalms 103:2, 3)

And meditating on the promises concerning prosperity builds faith for provision:

*But my God shall supply **all** your need according to his riches in glory by Christ Jesus.*
(Philippians 4:19)

For the LORD thy God bringeth thee into a good land,
*...thou **shalt not lack any thing** in it;*
 (Deuteronomy 8:7, 9)

And, my favorite, which covers almost anything else:

Delight thyself also in the LORD; and he shall give thee the desires of thine heart.
Commit thy way unto the LORD; trust also in him; and he shall bring it to pass. (Psalms 37:4)

Notice what the Lord said to Moses:

And all these blessings shall come on thee, and overtake thee, if thou shalt hearken unto the voice of the LORD thy God. (Deuteronomy 28:2)

Get that! "All these blessings shall come on you and **overtake** you" if you listen to the voice of the Lord your God.

I can testify that this is true. The more I spend time with Him, in His Word and in His Presence, the more He manifests His Goodness, His Love and His extravagant provision in my life.

When I am sick, He heals me. When I have a need, He provides it. When I started claiming "He renews my youth like the eagle" (Psalm 103:5) people started telling me I don't look my age, and I started having more energy and stamina. He even gives me the desires of my heart. And it keeps getting better every day.

And this is only the beginning. Look at these promises:

*And Jesus said unto them...: for verily I say unto you, If ye have faith as a grain of mustard seed, ye shall say unto this mountain, Remove hence to yonder place; and it shall remove; and **nothing shall be impossible unto you**.* (Matthew 17:20)

*For with God **nothing shall be impossible.**** (Luke 1:37)

*Verily, verily, I say unto you, He that believeth on me, **the works that I do shall he do also**; and greater works than these shall he do; because I go unto my Father.* (John 14:12)

*And **whatsoever ye shall ask in my name, that will I do**, that the Father may be glorified in the Son. **If ye shall ask any thing in my name, I will do it**.* (John 14:13, 14)

One day I said to the Lord "You just keep getting better and better!", and He replied, "No, I am always the same, you are just getting to know me better." (!)

Commit today to get to know your Heavenly Father by spending time with Him. It is not a chore; it is the greatest blessing you will ever receive. Being in His Presence is a greater joy than anything else He can give you, and He throws in everything else on top of it.

Jesus said, "It is the Father's good pleasure to give you the Kingdom". We know how much pleasure it gives us to bless our children. How much more pleasure does it give Our Father when we receive joyfully the bounty at His Hands and share His goodness with those around us.

Being enriched in every thing to all bountifulness, which causeth through us thanksgiving to God. (2Corinthians 9:11)

Surely we are blessed above all people. And what we have, we can share, with anyone who will receive. Our God has a limitless supply!

[All bolding author's emphasis]

Read the Manual

All scripture is given by inspiration of God, and is profitable for doctrine, for reproof, for correction, for instruction in righteousness: (2Timothy 3:1)6

At one time, I worked as a mechanical designer for a company that made the machines that make paper. These were huge machines that fit in a building about the size of a football field. When the machine was installed, the company that bought it was given a manual. When you buy a new car or appliance you are given a manual. The manufacturer wants to make sure that you know how to operate and maintain the product effectively so that it will perform the way it was intended to perform.

God created you in a certain manner and intends you to operate in a certain manner in order to insure best performance. He has given you a manual so that you can know how to maintain your life in order that it will function at peak performance. It is probably in a drawer or on a bookshelf gathering dust. This is what we usually do with manuals. Our manual is called "the Holy Bible".

In most manuals, there is a "hotline" number we can call when things break down or don't work properly. God has a "hotline" number also. Here it is: P-R-A-Y-E-R. When you call the hotline for an appliance, they will often refer you to a page in the manual. God often does that too. He will sometimes tell you to look at a certain passage of Scripture. I have many times in prayer had the Lord speak to my spirit and tell me to look at a particular passage. Or He may give me specific instructions, and with that instruction comes the Scripture passage that confirms it.

The Bible is more than a collection of words and ideas. Jesus said:

... the words that I speak unto you, they are spirit, and they are life. (John 6:63)

Notice He said His Word is "spirit" and "life".

Your spirit is the real you. It is the "you" that is created in the likeness and image of God. It requires a body to exist in this material realm on this earth, and it requires a soul (mind, will and emotions) to connect it to your body.

When your spirit returns to God who gave it (Ecclesiastes 12:7) your body dies.

The Bible itself, the Word of God, feeds and nourishes and strengthens your spirit as you read it. It also "restores your soul" (Psalm 23) and it contains instruction as to how to correctly maintain your body, which is the "temple" of God, as, if your are in Christ, He is living in you.

The answer to every problem of life is contained in the Scripture.

The Hebrew word for "word" *dabar* is also the Hebrew word for "thing" or "object".

The literal translation of Luke 1:37 is "No Word of God is without power".

This is one of the most powerful truths of the Word, if you can grasp it. The Word of God contains the power to perform what it says.

This is what the angel Gabriel was explaining when he answered Mary when she asked how could she conceive a child when she had not "known" a man.

Gabriel replied that her cousin Elizabeth had conceived a child when she was past childbearing age.

The way it had happened was the same way God would do it with Mary. He sent the angel Gabriel to "proclaim" the will of the Lord in her life and she received it and believed and it manifested.

Mary responded by doing the same thing. She received the Word of the Lord and believed. She said "Be it unto me according to thy Word".

God has given us His Word in the Scripture.

Examine the following passage:

> *For we have not followed cunningly devised fables, when we made known unto you the power and coming of our Lord Jesus Christ, but were eyewitnesses of his majesty.*
> *For he received from God the Father honour and glory, when there came such a voice to him from the excellent glory, This is my beloved Son, in whom I am well pleased.*
> *And this voice which came from heaven we heard, when we were with him in the holy mount.*
> *We have also a more sure word of prophecy; whereunto ye do well that ye take heed, as unto a light that shineth in a dark place, until the day dawn, and the day star arise in your hearts*: (2 Peter 1:16 - 19)

Let's "unpack" this. Peter is talking about the time that he, James and John were with Jesus when God the Father spoke from Heaven saying "This is my beloved Son, in whom I am well pleased."

He goes on to say that we have an even more "sure word of prophecy" than God speaking from

Heaven, and that is God's written Word the Scriptures.

When we receive the written Word as God's will and speak it and act as if we believe it is true, we release the power contained in the Word itself to manifest it in our lives.

For example, physical symptoms attack your body. You can either pick up the phone and call the doctor, or you can pick up the Bible and claim the scriptures pertaining to healing: "Jesus bore my sickness and my diseases and by His stripes I was healed"
(Matthew 8:17, 2 Peter 2:24)

When you get a bill you are not sure how you are going to pay, you begin to claim: "My God shall supply all my need according to His riches in glory through Christ Jesus". (Philippians 4:19)

But don't wait until the problem hits to build your faith. The faith to release into the situation comes from the Word.

"Faith comes by hearing, and hearing by the Word of God". (Romans 10:17)

Begin reading the Word daily to build and strengthen your faith so that when situations arise that you need to use it, you will have it ready.

If you buy a set of barbells to build your muscles and they sit on the floor, if a burglar comes into your house it won't do much good to go lift the barbells to get the strength to run him off.

Don't wait till the devil comes around to pick up the Word to run him off.

But, even greater than the provision that God has supplied in His Word is the joy that comes from His Presence alone.

Your desire follows your attention. If you have ever engaged in a sport or played a musical instrument, you know the more you practice, the more you enjoy it, the more you enjoy it, the more you practice. It is the same with God and His Word.

As you continue to read the Word, you will begin to feel as almost a physical sensation, the power of the Word flowing into your spirit bringing life and love, peace and joy.

"In His presence is fullness of joy"
(Psalm 16:11)

Overcoming Addiction

First of all, addiction is bondage. It may be to a substance, or a certain form of behavior or myriad other things. To understand it we must understand the root cause.

Please understand that the devil cannot create anything. All he can do is pervert what God has created to his own ends.

The Lord revealed to me when I was writing my book, <u>Christianity Made Simple</u>, that man is "addictive" by nature. We were created to be "addicted", if you will, to the presence of God. David speaks of it here:

As the hart panteth after the water brooks, so panteth my soul after thee, O God. My soul thirsteth for God, for the living God...
(Psalms 42:1, 2)

O God, thou art my God; early will I seek thee: my soul thirsteth for thee, my flesh longeth for thee in a dry and thirsty land, where no water is; To see thy power and thy glory...(Psalms 63:1, 2)

What David is describing here is worship. We were created with a need to worship God; to be in His presence and experience the fullness of His love, to be filled with His peace and to allow Him to permeate us with His nature so that "rivers of living water" may flow out of our "innermost being". (John 7:38)

From the time our spirit leaves the Father's presence and takes up residence on this earth (Ecclesiastes 12:7), we are consumed with a driving need for the Father's love. This is why babies must be held. They have found in orphanages that babies who are fed and warm but were not held and loved do not thrive. Children who are loved grow up with a sense of security which sustains them, and children who are not given the nurturing and love necessary for security tend to seek consolation in dangerous ways and have difficulty receiving love. All true love is from God. He *is* love. (1 John 4:8) It is the love of the Father that our spirits seek.

Paul expresses it here:

But we all, with open face beholding as in a glass the glory of the Lord, are changed into the same image from glory to glory, even as by the Spirit of the Lord. (2 Corinthians 3:18)

Notice it says "we are changed into His image", the image of Christ, as we "behold His glory".

We were created to be "addicted" to being in His presence, where He changes us from "glory to glory" into His image, and His goodness and mercy and grace will flow to us and through us to all we meet. In His presence is fullness of joy, and provision of every need, healing, protection, prosperity, and peace. In actual fact the Hebrew word for "peace", *shalom,* means "nothing missing, nothing broken".

If we do not satisfy this God-longing as He intended, we will try to satisfy it with something else. This "something else" becomes our "god". It may be something good in itself, work, a sport, a skill, the internet - Hello (!); in which case it will take on a distorted importance in our lives. Or it may be something dangerous, a substance or an ungodly relationship. In all these instances it will eventually become destructive. This is the reason why people stay in abusive relationships. This is why addictions are so difficult to control. This driving, powerful force, which is designed to keep us in the love of God, is perverted to keep us in the grip of whatever thing we have erected in His place. It has become an "idol".

Examine your life and evaluate where your focus is. What motivates you? This is your God.

There is only one true cure for addiction; we must put God on the throne of our lives where He belongs. This only happens by accepting His Son, Jesus Christ.

If the Son therefore shall make you free, ye shall be free indeed. (John 8:36)

When we make a whole-hearted, sincere commitment to serve Jesus and allow Him to become the "Lord" of our lives, when we determine with all our hearts to turn from whatever is not pleasing to Him and obey Him in all things, when we come into His presence with hearts open wide to allow Him to fill us with His, love, truth, peace and joy, He will transform our lives and change us "into His image, from glory to glory, by the Spirit of the Lord".

Only Jesus can transform our lives into what God intended them to be. It is only in the presence of the Father of Life, the Creator of the Universe, that we find the joy, fulfillment and power to live a holy life, sanctified for the Father's purpose, that the Holy Spirit may fill us with His power and His glory to transform our lives and flow through us as "rivers of living waters" to touch and transform the lives of those around us bringing Heaven to Earth, that our days may be, as God intended, "days of Heaven on Earth". (Deuteronomy 11:21)

If you have never experienced the transforming power of God, the presence of the Holy Spirit and the perfect love of the Father of Life, just come alone into a private place and pray this prayer out loud, with an open heart, commit your life to Him and prepare to walk with Him, spending time daily in prayer and in His Word, obeying His voice and His written Word, and watch Him transform your life - moment by moment, day by day - and touch the lives of those around you with His love,.

Precious Father of life and love, I come to you in the Name of your Son Jesus Christ, thanking you for your love in giving Him as a ransom for my life. I repent of all I have done walking against your will and living contrary to your plan for my life. I place my life in your hands, totally trusting you and determining to obey you wherever you lead in every area of my life. Take my life and make it pleasing to you, a living sacrifice to the glory of Jesus' name, and use me to bring your love to the people around me. Please come to me, with your power and your glory, and fill me with your love and power. Please help me to hear your voice and follow none other. I thank you that you are faithful, and you will do it according to your precious promises. In Jesus' Name.

Then just spend time in His presence loving Him and experiencing Him. He is faithful, He will meet you there. I am agreeing in prayer that everyone who reads this article will experience the powerful, life-changing, perfect and beautiful love of the Father in a new and powerful way.

Nothing on earth can ever compare to His boundless love and glory. He is the end of all desire, He satisfies every need, He fills us to overflowing, until we have only one desire, to share all he has given us with anyone who will receive.

Praise His Name forever!

The Battle is the Lord's

...for the battle is the LORD'S, (1 Samuel 17:47)

These words were spoken by David as he faced the giant, Goliath. We all know what happened then - He won!

Are you in a battle today? I doubt there is anyone alive today who is not facing some sort of battle - finances, illness, relationships... Everyone seems to be dealing with more than they can handle.

If this is you, take heart; there is an answer that is bigger than your problem. His name is Jesus.

I like this story in the book of Joshua. "A great multitude" was gathered against Judah so they proclaimed a fast and sought the Lord to know what to do.

Then there came some that told Jehoshaphat, saying, There cometh a great multitude against thee from beyond the sea on this side Syria; ...
And Jehoshaphat feared, and set himself to seek the LORD, and proclaimed a fast throughout all Judah.

And Judah gathered themselves together, to ask help of the LORD: even out of all the cities of Judah they came to seek the LORD
(2 Chronicles 20:2 - 4)

And this is what the Lord told them:

Ye shall not need to fight in this battle: set yourselves, stand ye still, and see the salvation of the LORD with you, O Judah and Jerusalem: fear not, nor be dismayed; to morrow go out against them: for the LORD will be with you.
(2 Chronicles 20:17)

Notice the Lord said "You will not need to fight in this battle... for the Lord is with you".

Then look what happened:

And they rose early in the morning, and went forth into the wilderness of Tekoa: and as they went forth, Jehoshaphat stood and said, Hear me, O Judah, and ye inhabitants of Jerusalem; Believe in the LORD your God, so shall ye be established; believe his prophets, so shall ye prosper.
And when he had consulted with the people, he appointed singers unto the LORD, and that should praise the beauty of holiness, as they went out before the army, and to say, Praise the LORD; for his mercy endureth for ever.

And when they began to sing and to praise, the LORD set ambushments against the children of Ammon, Moab, and mount Seir, which were come against Judah; and they were smitten.

For the children of Ammon and Moab stood up against the inhabitants of mount Seir, utterly to slay and destroy them: and when they had made an end of the inhabitants of Seir, every one helped to destroy another.

And when Judah came toward the watch tower in the wilderness, they looked unto the multitude, and, behold, they were dead bodies fallen to the earth, and none escaped.

And when Jehoshaphat and his people came to take away the spoil of them, they found among them in abundance both riches with the dead bodies, and precious jewels, which they stripped off for themselves, more than they could carry away: and they were three days in gathering of the spoil, it was so much.

And on the fourth day they assembled themselves in the valley of Berachah [prosperity]; for there they blessed the LORD: therefore the name of the same place was called, The valley of Berachah, unto this day.

Then they returned, every man of Judah and Jerusalem, and Jehoshaphat in the forefront of them, to go again to Jerusalem with joy; for the

LORD had made them to rejoice over their enemies. (2 Chronicles 20 - 27)

Here we see the pattern for receiving God's deliverance. Notice they first appointed singers and praisers that they should "praise the beauty of holiness" before the Lord. As they began to praise God in the midst of their circumstances, the Lord "set ambushments" against the enemy and they returned "with joy: for the Lord had made them to rejoice over their enemies" because "the Lord fought against" their enemies. Not only did the Lord win the battle for them, but it took three days for them to gather in the "spoils".

God will always do "exceeding abundantly more than we can think or ask"! (Ephesians 3:20)

But, be sure to remember, our enemies are not people.

For we wrestle not against flesh and blood, but against principalities, against powers, against the rulers of the darkness of this world, against spiritual wickedness in high places. (Ephesians 6:12)

Our enemies are the spirits of darkness that hold people bound in deception. They do not know why they do what they do. This is why we are commanded to pray for our enemies. They need deliverance, too.

Notice this Scripture:

Out of the mouth of babes and sucklings hast thou ordained strength because of thine enemies, that thou mightest still the enemy and the avenger. (Psalms 8:2)

When Jesus quoted this passage as recorded in the gospel of Matthew it is translated this way:

And Jesus saith unto them, "Yea; have ye never read, Out of the mouth of babes and sucklings thou hast perfected praise?" (Matthew 21:16)

So we can more accurately translate Psalm 8:2 as: "… God has perfected praise, that He might still (stop) the enemy and the avenger".

Praise stops the enemy! Praise is powerful. Praise is the most powerful thing we can do. When we stop in the middle of our circumstances to just focus on Jesus and praise Him for what He has done on the cross, we release His power and His Glory to come on the scene and change our circumstances. But, before we even see the results in the circumstances, we will feel the result in our spirit as faith arises in our hearts with the confidence that our God is bigger than any circumstance the devil can bring our way.

But thou art holy, O thou that inhabitest the praises of Israel. (Psalms 22:3)

Wow! Is that powerful! God "inhabits" our praise.

71

When we praise God in the midst of our trouble God "arises". And what happens when God arises?

Let God arise, let his enemies be scattered: let them also that hate him flee before him.
(Psalms 68:1)

When God arises, His enemies are scattered and flee before Him.

So let your praises flow and watch God arise and scatter your enemies.

Don't know what to say? Start with just thanking Jesus for what He has done. Thank Him for being willing to go to the cross on your behalf and purchasing your redemption from death and hell. Thank Him for making you free. Thank Him in advance for what He has already done on your behalf to change your current circumstances. Praise Him for His faithfulness, goodness and truth. As you continue the words will begin to flow, and faith and joy will begin to arise in your heart as you know that He is in control, His Word is truth and He will never fail you or forsake you.

"The battle is the Lord's," and He has already won.

The Integrity of God's Word

In the beginning was the Word, and the Word was with God, and the Word was God.
(John 1:1)

Notice "the Word was God". God and His Word are one. You cannot separate them. The original Greek version of Luke 1:37 is, literally, *"No word of God is without power".*

Through faith we understand that the worlds were framed by the word of God, so that things which are seen were not made of things which do appear. (Hebrews 11:3)

The author of Hebrews also says;

"He [God] *is upholding all things by the word of His power".* (Hebrews 1:3)

So God's Word is upholding all things.

It is interesting that quantum physics now shows us that sound frequencies are contained in everything.

We need to get the revelation of the power of God's Word. When we speak God's Word in faith, believing and not doubting, it has the same power as it did when it proceeded from the mouth of God and the universe sprang into being.

Jesus said *"The words that I speak they are spirit and they are life"*. (John 6:63)

It is essential to get the revelation of the power of the Word of God in order to receive the promises of God.

God said "Light be" and light was. (Genesis 1:3) So we see the world was created by the power of God's Word. He then created man in His own image. (Genesis 1:26, 27) Animals have the power of communication by "speech", but only humans have the creative power of God in their words.

Death and life are in the power of the tongue: and they that love it shall eat the fruit thereof. (Proverbs 18:21)

To "eat the fruit of" means to "bear the consequences". In other words, what we say will produce results, either positive or negative, depending on what we say.

Recall what Jesus said:

For verily I say unto you, That whosoever shall say unto this mountain, Be thou removed, and be thou cast into the sea; and shall not doubt in his heart, but shall believe that those things which he saith shall come to pass; he shall have whatsoever he saith. (Mark 11:23)

The life we are living today is a result of what we spoke into it yesterday. If we want to change our circumstances, we have to change what we are saying. But we must also "believe what we say will come to pass". In other words, we have to have the revelation of the power of our words.

How do we come to the place where we can always say what we want, rather than what we have, or fear, and have the conviction that what we say will come to pass? By getting the revelation of the truth and power of the Word of God and making our Words line up with His Word, so that what we speak has the power of God's Word behind it.

How do we discipline ourselves to speak and believe his Word? By keeping it before our eyes and in our hearts, until it governs what comes from our mouths.

My son, attend to my words; incline thine ear unto my sayings.

Let them not depart from thine eyes; keep them in the midst of thine heart.

For they are life unto those that find them, and health to all their flesh.
(Proverbs 4:20 - 22)

This book of the law shall not depart out of thy mouth; but thou shalt meditate therein day and night, that thou mayest observe to do according to all that is written therein; for then thou shalt make thy way prosperous, and then thou shalt have good success. (Joshua 1:8)

Notice, we are told we must keep the Word before our eyes and in our hearts.

for out of the abundance of the heart the mouth speaks. (Matthew12:34)

This is Jesus speaking here. He said the mouth speaks what the heart is filled with. If we want to speak the Word of God into our lives, we must fill our hearts with it.

You say "Well that sounds like it will take a lot of time", and you are right. But do you have time to lay in bed sick? Do you have time to correct the mistakes you make when you do not allow God to lead you moment by moment so you can have "good success".

Once you begin taking the time to fill your heart and mind with the Word of God, you will find it pays off in dividends you could never have imagined.

76

A well-known healing evangelist got this revelation early on in his ministry. The Lord told him if he would read the gospels and the book of Acts four times in a month he would get a revelation of Jesus that would empower his ministry. He did and it did. When I heard this, I decided I would do the same. I had been struggling in faith in some areas in my life. I know the Word is true, and I know God is faithful, but I would find myself figuring out ways to fix things myself if God didn't answer (!) This is not faith; it is called "worrying".

When I made the decision to read the first five books of the New Testament four times in a month, I divided the number of pages by 30 and read that many pages a day. When I got halfway through the book of Mark I suddenly realized that a transformation had taken place. I was no longer finding myself worrying; I would just become overwhelmed with the love of God several times a day and have to take time to thank Him for showing me his faithfulness and goodness. I began to see answers to things I had been "standing in faith" for years to see.

Another wonderful benefit of spending this much time in the Word is the joy that comes from being in the presence of God.

Thou wilt shew me the path of life: in thy presence is fulness of joy; at thy right hand there are pleasures for evermore. (Psalm 16:11)

77

"Fulness of joy"!   You can't get any more joy
than that!

Make a quality decision to take God at His Word
and press in to receive all He has prepared for
you since "before the foundation of the world".
Determine to quit living below your potential in
Him, and to quit limiting His boundless
resources in your life.   When you do, you will
bring glory to him and blessing to those around
you.

*Shout for joy and be glad...Let the LORD be
magnified, which hath pleasure in the prosperity
of his servant.* (Psalm 35:27)

*Fear not, little flock; for it is your Father's good
pleasure to give you the kingdom.* (Luke 12:32)

*Therefore shall ye lay up these my words in your
heart and in your soul, ...*
*That your days may be multiplied, and the days
of your children,... **as the days of heaven upon
the earth**.* (Deuteronomy 11:18 - 21)

You Are Healed

Bless the LORD, O my soul…who healeth all thy diseases; (Psalm 103:2, 3)

God is the only one who ever finished before He began. Time only exists in this dimension. In God, everything is eternal. (2 Corinthians 4:16) Before He created the world by speaking it into existence, it was already complete. Everything you need or ever will need has already been provided in Him. (2 Peter 1:3) He knew your end before your beginning. (Psalms 139:16).

God spoke the world into existence. He said (literally in the Hebrew) "Light be!" and light was. (Genesis 1:3) He then created man in His own image. The same creative power that flows forth when God speaks inhabits the words of man. Unfortunately, most people are unaware of the power of their words, so they are speaking things into their lives that they really don't want to have.

Death and life are in the power of the tongue: and they that love it shall eat the fruit thereof. (Proverbs 18:21)

Once we get hold of this principle, we can change our lives by the power of God's Word. Jesus said:

"Whosoever says to that mountain be cast into the sea, and doubt not in his heart, but believes the thing he says will come to pass will have whatsoever he says" (Mark 11:23)

Notice He said "whosoever" will have "whatsoever" he says, not "certain special people" will have "certain special things".

We must be careful to always say what we want, not what is. The Bible tells us God "calls the things that be not as though they are". (Romans 4:17) In other words, God creates by speaking what He wants to happen, not what already is. We tend to say what is, not what should be.

Your words are indicators for your future. When you get on an elevator, you push the button for the floor you want to go to. If you push the button for the floor you are on, you stay in the same place.

Your words are like the elevator button. If you confess "I am sick", you will stay sick. If you feed your heart on God's Word that says "Jesus bore your sickness and your pain, and by His wounds you are healed", (Isaiah 53: 4,5; Matthew 8:17; I Peter 2:24) speaking only that word continually, without doubting or speaking contradiction, God's healing will manifest in your body.

God's Word says He has already provided all things that pertain to life and godliness by the knowledge of Him and who He is.

*According as his divine power hath given unto us all things that pertain unto life and godliness, through the knowledge of him that hath called us to glory and virtue: (*2Peter 1:3)

Everything we ever can want or need has already been provided through Jesus' death, resurrection and ascension. By faith in Him we can receive forgiveness, healing, prosperity, eternal life, and most of all, fellowship with Him and the Father. This fellowship and living in His presence is the source of all joy. Many people are seeking joy in so many places and it is so simple. Come to the Father of life and joy through His Son, Jesus.

What Jesus did on the cross was an exchange.

• He took our sin to give us His righteousness.

For he hath made him to be sin for us, who knew no sin; that we might be made the righteousness of God in him. (2 Corinthians 5:21)

• He took our sickness to give us divine health.

Himself took our infirmities, and bare our sicknesses... by whose stripes ye were healed. (Matthew 8:16,17, I Peter 2:24, Isaiah 53:5)

• He took our poverty to give us divine prosperity.

For ye know the grace of our Lord Jesus Christ, that, though he was rich, yet for your sakes he became poor, that ye through his poverty might be rich. (2 Corinthians 8:9)

• He took our death to give us eternal life

For God so loved the world, that he gave his only begotten Son, that whosoever believeth in him should not perish, but have everlasting life. (John 3:16)

• He took our rejection to make us God's children.

But as many as received him, to them gave he power to become the sons of God... (John 1:12)

We receive all these things through faith in Christ. The Jewish New Testament (translated by Jewish Christians or "Messianic" Jews) translates this word "faith" as "trust". This is easier to understand. We can make a decision to trust. When we decide to trust God, and trust His Word, which says He provides all our needs including healing, and we make our words line up with His Word, the Bible tells us "I will hasten [Hebrew; *shâqad 'al* "watch over"] my Word to bring it to pass". (Jeremiah 1:12) We will soon see our lives line up with His Word. But we must be consistent, and speak only those things we want to see come to pass.

When the doctor gives us a bad report, we can accept it and go tell our friends how sick we are and how long we must put up with it, according to what the doctor says, or we can say "Jesus bore my sickness and my diseases and by His wounds I am healed." (1 Peter 2:24, Matthew 8:16, 17) and continue to thank Him for it until we see it manifest in our body.

The faith to believe without doubting comes from reading the Word, having it before your eyes, speaking it with your mouth, and not saying anything to contradict it.

My son, attend to my words; incline thine ear unto my sayings.

Let them not depart from thine eyes; keep them in the midst of thine heart.
For they are life unto those that find them, and health to all their flesh. (Proverbs 4:20 - 22)

For as the rain cometh down, and the snow from heaven, and returneth not thither, but watereth the earth, and maketh it bring forth and bud, that it may give seed to the sower, and bread to the eater:
So shall my word be that goeth forth out of my mouth: it shall not return unto me void, but it shall accomplish that which I please, and it shall prosper in the thing whereto I sent it.
(Isaiah 55:10,11)

God's Word will accomplish what it was sent to do.

Always remember, God loves you, He is good and everything from Him is good. Anything that is not good is not from God. Sickness is not from God.

Bless the LORD, O my soul, and forget not all his benefits:
... who healeth <u>all</u> thy diseases; (Psalm 103:2)

The thief cometh not, but for to steal, and to kill, and to destroy: I am come that they might have life, and that they might have it more abundantly. (John 10:10)

...for I am the LORD that healeth thee.
(Exodus 15:26)

Jesus paid a terrible price for your healing.

Healing belongs to you. Receive it in Jesus' Name

Heaven on Earth

Therefore shall ye lay up these my words in your heart and in your soul, and bind them for a sign upon your hand, that they may be as frontlets between your eyes.

And ye shall teach them your children, speaking of them when thou sittest in thine house, and when thou walkest by the way, when thou liest down, and when thou risest up.

And thou shalt write them upon the door posts of thine house, and upon thy gates:

That your days may be multiplied, and the days of your children, in the land which the LORD sware unto your fathers to give them, as the days of heaven upon the earth.
(Deuteronomy 11:18 - 21)

This is God's promise to Moses for the Children of Isreal if they would honor His Word and obey Him. This is the blessing of the Old Covenant. Notice He said "That your days may be... as the days of heaven upon the earth". And we have a new and even "better covenant"! (Hebrews 8:6)

Notice we see Jesus telling the disciples to pray, "Thy kingdom come, thy will be done, on earth as it is in Heaven".

So we have it again, "on earth, as it is in heaven" or "heaven on earth".

This is the idea of the Kingdom of God. This is the inheritance of the "saints of light" or those who have become children in the "family of God " through faith in Christ.

But as many as received him, to them gave he power to become the sons of God, even to them that believe on his name: (John 1:12)

Religion has watered down the truth of the gospel and turned it around to the point where it is no longer "days of heaven on earth", but only going to heaven once you die.

Jesus said, in effect, that the traditions of men make the Word of God ineffectual.

And he said unto them, Full well ye reject the commandment of God, that ye may keep your own tradition. ...making the word of God of none effect through your tradition, (Mark 7:9 - 13)

The power of the truth of the gospel, which was intended to spread the Kingdom of God, thereby bringing "Heaven to Earth", has been watered down to the message of simply eventually going to heaven when you die.

Please read the gospels and see if ever Jesus went around telling people "Be of good cheer, in this world you have to be sick and poor and miserable, but when you get to heaven you will be happy".

No, he healed the sick, delivered the oppressed, multiplied the bread and fish to feed the hungry, he blessed the livelihood of the fishermen, He even raised the dead.

And then He told the disciples: *"As my father has sent me, so send I you"*. (John 20:21)

He also said:

"Verily, verily, I say unto you, He that believeth on me, the works that I do shall he do also; and greater works than these shall he do; because I go unto my Father." (John 14:12)

He said, furthermore,

If thou canst believe, all things are possible to him that believeth. (Mark 9:23)

"If you can believe". Here is the essence of receiving the Kingdom of God to the extent that our days may be "days of Heaven on Earth". If you can believe...

If you believe that the most you can expect is to go to Heaven when you die, and you are maybe not really sure of that, what you need is an intensive study of God's Word to get to know your Heavenly Father and know His perfect will for you as His child, the apple of His eye.

The apostle Peter said:

According as his divine power hath given unto us all things that pertain unto life and godliness, through the knowledge of him that hath called us to glory and virtue: (2 Peter 1:3)

Notice "his divine power hath [has already] given us all things that pertain to life and godliness".

So God has already given us everything we need. But we have to receive them. How do we receive them?

Peter goes on to say "through the knowledge of him". Of whom? Of God.

So we learn to receive what God has provided by learning to know Him.

How do we learn to know Him? By spending time in His Word, and meditating on His promises, and spending time in His Presence, just worshipping Him and fellowshipping with Him, until His Word is the driving force in our lives, consuming our thoughts and flowing from our mouths.

Jesus said:

If ye abide in me, and my words abide in you, ye shall ask what ye will, and it shall be done unto you. (John 15:7)

Here we have it. If we "abide" in Him, spend time with Him, acknowledge His presence constantly in all we think, say and do, and spend time in His Word so that His Word "abides" in us, whatever we ask Him to do He will do.

This is faith - having the confidence that whatever we have asked is done.

Notice what Jesus says here:

Therefore I say unto you, What things soever ye desire, when ye pray, believe that ye receive them, and ye shall have them. (Mar 11:24)

"When you pray, believe that you receive", not "Believe it when you see it", but "When you pray, believe that you receive".

As the apostle John put it:

For whatsoever is born of God overcometh the world:
...and this is the victory that overcometh the world, even our faith. (I John 5:4)

Recall, Jesus said:

These things I have spoken unto you, that in me ye might have peace. In the world ye shall have tribulation: but be of good cheer; I have overcome the world. (John 16:33)

Yes, we have tribulation in this world. But "Be of good cheer", Jesus has overcome the world. And through Him, in the power of His Name, through the power of His Word, through faith in His Word, and his accomplished work on the Cross, so have we.

We are to "reign in life" (Romans 5:17), as overcomers, doing the works that Jesus does and destroying the works of the devil.

He that believeth on me, the works that I do shall he do also; (John 14:12)

For this purpose the Son of God was manifested, that he might destroy the works of the devil.
(I John 3:8)

*Behold, I give unto you power to tread on serpents and scorpions, and over **all** the power of the enemy:* (Luke 10:19)

Arise and put on Christ (Galatians 3:27) and walk out your destiny in Him, taking authority over the circumstances in your life and bringing the light of the gospel of Christ to those around you with the Good News that Jesus is alive, He is living in you, and He has come to set them free - not just from death, but from poverty, sickness and all the works of the devil.

The Baptism in the Holy Spirit

John the Baptist was in Jerusalem baptizing and preaching, saying, "Repent for the Kingdom of Heaven is at hand". And, he said;

I indeed baptize you with water unto repentance: but he that cometh after me is mightier than I, whose shoes I am not worthy to bear: he shall baptize you with the Holy Ghost, and with fire. (Matthew 3:11)

He was speaking of Jesus saying that Jesus would baptize with the Holy Ghost and with fire. After Jesus rose from the dead, He told the disciples,

"Tarry ye in the city of Jerusalem, until ye be endued with power from on high." (Luke 24:49)

They were to wait in Jerusalem until they received "power from on high".

Later we read;

And when the day of Pentecost was fully come, they were all with one accord in one place.

And suddenly there came a sound from heaven as of a rushing mighty wind, and it filled all the

And there appeared unto them cloven tongues like as of fire, and it sat upon each of them.

And they were <u>all filled with the Holy Ghost</u>, and began to speak with other tongues, as the Spirit gave them utterance, (Acts 2:1,4)

Here we see the event that John the Baptist was speaking of when He said that Jesus would "baptize with the Holy Ghost and with fire". The Scripture tells us here that there appeared what looked like "tongues of fire" on each one of them and they were "all filled with the Holy Ghost". Notice the result that they all "began to speak with other tongues, as the Spirit gave them utterance" or as the Holy Spirit gave them the words to speak.

God has not changed. Everything He did in those days, He is still doing now. But we have to receive by faith. Notice the appearance of "tongues of fire" sat on <u>each</u> of them, they were <u>all</u> filled with the Holy Ghost and the wording indicates that they <u>all</u> began to speak with other tongues.

This is not surprising. Let's look again at Jesus final words to the disciples:

And these signs shall follow them that believe; In my name shall they cast out devils; they shall speak with new tongues. (Mark 16:17)

He says these signs shall follow "them that believe". Not just a few chosen special people, but "them that believe". Do you believe? If you do, then this means you.

Here is another reference to this phenomenon. Peter was preaching to some people gathered at the house of Cornelius, a Roman centurion, and as He was speaking the Bible tells us "the Holy Ghost fell on all them that heard the Word". It goes on to say that the Jews were astonished that the Holy Ghost had been poured out on the Gentiles [A Gentile was anyone who was not a Jew. Up until this time all the believers had been Jews]. How did they know the Holy Ghost had been poured out on the Gentiles? It says very clearly:

For they heard them speak with tongues, and magnify God (Acts 10:46)

So, we see that "speaking with tongues", or speaking in a language which one hasn't learned (often referred to as a "prayer language" or "heavenly language") is a sign that one has received the Holy Spirit.

We don't hear a lot about this publicly today, and perhaps this is the first time you have heard of it.   But, we can clearly see that this is something that God desires for us.

I want to mention here that many times people think that because they may not have heard of miraculous things taking place that the supernatural things that happened in the early church were only for then and that God just isn't doing these things any more. This could not be farther from the truth. It is beyond the scope of this book to recount the miracles that are taking place in our world today, which you don't hear about in the secular media, but be assured God hasn't changed.

God tells us through the prophet Malachi,

For I the LORD change not   (Malachi 3:6)

Also, the writer to the Hebrews writes;

Jesus Christ the same yesterday, and today, and forever. (Hebrews 13:8)

Jesus hasn't changed.   What He did two thousand years ago He still does.

Jesus told all the disciples to tarry (wait) in Jerusalem until they would receive power from on high.   Was this the first time they had received the Holy Spirit?

No, it wasn't. We see that after Jesus rose from the dead and he appeared to the disciples, the Bible tells us He breathed on them and said, *"Receive the Holy Ghost"*. (John 20:22) So they had already received the Holy Ghost, yet Jesus told them to wait in Jerusalem until they would receive "power from on high".

Why was that? Well, when we are born again, the Holy Spirit takes up residence on the inside of us to live within us and transform us into the likeness of Christ, if we will yield to His leading and allow Him to do this.

But the Baptism in the Holy Spirit is an empowering for ministry. The word "baptism" comes from the same Greek word we saw earlier, *bap-tid'-zo*, which means to immerse, or to make fully wet. I have heard one Bible teacher describe it this way. When we are born again, we receive the spirit "within" us, and when we are baptized in the Holy Spirit, we receive the spirit "upon" us. The spirit "within" separates us from the world into Christ. But the spirit "upon" us empowers us to serve Him.

Let's examine this account of the apostle Paul:

Paul having passed through the upper coasts came to Ephesus:
and finding certain disciples,
He said unto them, Have ye received the Holy Ghost since ye believed? And they said unto

him, We have not so much as heard whether there be any Holy Ghost.

And he said unto them, Unto what then were ye baptized? And they said, Unto John's baptism.

Then said Paul, John verily baptized with the baptism of repentance, saying unto the people, that they should believe on him which should come after him, that is, on Christ Jesus.

When they heard this, they were baptized in the name of the Lord Jesus.

And when Paul had laid his hands upon them, the Holy Ghost came on them; and they spake with tongues, and prophesied.

(Acts 19:1,6)

Notice here that when Paul asked them if they had received the Holy Ghost they told him they had never heard of the Holy Ghost. They hadn't even heard of Jesus but had been baptized into John's baptism. When Paul explained Jesus to them, they were baptized in the Name of Jesus and then *afterwards* Paul laid his hands on them and it tells us the "Holy Ghost came on them" and they spoke with tongues and prophesied.

When we are "baptized in the Holy Spirit", we are empowered to operate in what the Bible refers to as the "gifts" of the spirit. These gifts are listed as follows:

*For to one is given by the Spirit the word of
wisdom; to another the word of knowledge
by the same Spirit;*

*To another faith by the same Spirit; to another
the gifts of healing by the same Spirit;*

*To another the working of miracles; to another
prophecy; to another discerning of spirits;
to another divers kinds of tongues; to
another the interpretation of tongues.*
(I Corinthians 12:8-10)

I will briefly describe these gifts. They are
divided loosely into three categories, which are
sometimes referred to as the vocal gifts, the
power gifts and the gifts of revelation.

The vocal gifts are "divers [different] kinds of
tongues [languages]", "interpretation of
tongues", and "prophecy".

I want to distinguish here between what is being
referred to here as "Divers kinds of tongues" and
the prayer language or "unknown" tongue, which
you receive when you first receive the baptism in
the Holy Spirit. The prayer language you first
receive is always accessible. Once you have
received it, you can pray in it at any time, as you
will. The Holy Spirit will give you the words to
pray in your "unknown tongue" any time you
chose to yield to Him. It is up to you.

This is such a powerful and important gift I will
discuss it in depth in the following chapter. As

we have mentioned it is a person speaking in a language they haven't learned as the Holy Spirit gives them utterance" (Acts 2:4) or, rather as the Holy Spirit gives them the words to say. A person operating in this manifestation is praying out God's plan for his own or others' lives, as directed by the Holy Spirit.

The gift of "divers tongues" or "different languages" spoken of here refers to a person given an "utterance" in an unknown tongue in the church which is God speaking through the individual to the church. It is the Holy Spirit speaking *through* one believer to another or others.

"Interpretation of tongues" is not literal translation, or knowing word-for-word what is said, as one does when translating a known language, but it is rather a supernatural impartation of the knowledge of the sense of what is being said by the person speaking in tongues to the listener, to whom the language spoken is also unknown.

"Prophecy" means, literally, to "tell forth" or predict. It is a supernatural speaking forth of events that are to happen. It can also be a clarification of events that are happening and a revelation of God's will pertaining to certain situations. This is usually God speaking to the church, as opposed to the "word of wisdom" which is often to an individual.

The "revelation gifts" are the "word of knowledge", "word of wisdom" and the "discerning of spirits".

The "word of knowledge" is when a person is given revelation of an event that has occurred in the past, frequently regarding another individual, which facilitates ministry to that individual.

The "word of wisdom" is revelation of an event that is going to occur in the future, or guidance or direction pertaining to a course of action that will affect future events, usually for an individual.

"Discerning of spirits" is just what it sounds like. It is the ability to discern what spirits are affecting a given situation in order that we can take authority over them in prayer.

The "power" gifts are the gifts of "healing", "miracles" and "faith".

The gift of "healing" is just what it says. It is supernatural healing of sickness and disease, usually gradual, but sometimes sudden.

The gift of "miracles" is a spontaneous supernatural intervention in natural events. It may also be a miraculously manifested healing. We are beginning to hear of many "creative" miracles recently where God is replacing lost limbs and organs.

The gift of "faith" is miraculous faith, or a superabundant faith. It is supercharged faith that brings ones ability to believe to a dramatically higher level.

These are VERY brief introductory descriptions of these gifts. An intense study of these gifts is beyond the scope of this book, but there are many books and materials available to study them in greater depth.

I particularly want to point out here that while the nine gifts of the Spirit as listed above are manifested as the Spirit wills (I Corinthians 12:11), the ability to "pray in tongues" is available to anyone who receives the Baptism of the Holy Spirit to utilize at his own will, whenever one chooses. The only choice you have regarding the nine gifts listed above is whether or not to yield to the Holy Spirit and allow Him to manifest them through you. You can refuse to yield to Him, but you cannot force Him to move.

The other vital benefit for a new believer receiving the Baptism of the Holy Spirit is that the Scriptures come alive as the Holy Spirit enables your understanding to comprehend them. This is only logical, as the Bible tells us that the Scriptures were written by men who were "moved by the Holy Spirit" (II Peter 1:21). In other words, it was the Holy Spirit who wrote the Scripture, what better teacher to help you to understand them.

As a matter of fact, the Bible tells us exactly that.

But the anointing which ye have received of him abideth in you, and ye need not that any man teach you: but as the same anointing teacheth you of all things, and is truth, and is no lie, and even as it hath taught you, ye shall abide in him. (I John 2:27)

What John is saying here is that the "anointing" which you have received [the Holy Spirit] lives in you, and you do not need any man to teach you, but the Holy Spirit will teach you all things.

Jesus said the same thing.

Howbeit when he, the Spirit of truth, is come, he will guide you into all truth: for he shall not speak of himself; but whatsoever he shall hear, that shall he speak: and he will show you things to come.
(John 16:13)

Jesus is saying here that the "Spirit of truth", or the Holy Spirit, will guide you into all truth.

This is such an awesome revelation here. You often hear people use the term the "secret of life", usually in jest, because most people don't really believe there is any such thing. But what we are talking about here is truly the "secret of life".

The secret of the LORD is with them that fear him.(Psalm 25:14)

We can have an intimate relationship with the Creator of the Universe and He wants to guide us into "all truth". I can't imagine anything more worth having than that.

You are probably wondering, "OK, so I pray and believe to receive this 'baptism in the Holy Spirit' and I pray and something I can't understand comes out. How do I know that is the Holy Spirit giving me the words?"

Jesus answered that question for us too. He said,

> *If a son shall ask bread of any of you that is a father, will he give him a stone? or if he ask a fish, will he for a fish give him a serpent?*
> *Or if he shall ask an egg, will he offer him a scorpion?*
> *If ye then, being evil, know how to give good gifts unto your children: how much more shall your heavenly Father give the Holy Spirit to them that ask him?*
> (Luke 11:11-13)

I believe He was answering this question here. He is saying if we ask for bread [bread is symbolic for the word of God] our Heavenly

Father will not give us a stone. The words we speak, believing the Holy Spirit (who is God) to be speaking through us, will in fact be His Words, and not anything else. He goes on to say that if we ask for fish, he will not give us a serpent, and if we ask for an egg, he will not give us a scorpion. Then he says, "How much more will he give the Holy Spirit to them that ask him?" I think we can take His Word for it that when we ask for the Holy Spirit, we can be sure that is what we will get.

They Spoke in "Other Tongues"

And when the day of Pentecost was fully come,
they were all with one accord in one place.
And suddenly there came a sound from heaven
as of a rushing mighty wind, and it filled all
the house where they were sitting.
And there appeared unto them cloven tongues
like as of fire, and it sat upon each of them.
And they were all filled with the Holy Ghost, and
began to speak with other tongues, as the
Spirit gave them utterance. (Acts 2:1-4)

We see that when the Holy Spirit first fell and
filled believers He manifested Himself by
causing them to speak in other "tongues" or
languages. Why did God do it this way? Many
of us have asked that question over the years.

I believe the answer can be found in the Epistle
of James. He tells us,

If any man among you seem to be religious, and
bridleth not his tongue, but deceiveth his
own heart, this man's religion is vain.
(James 1:26)

107

The Greek word *khal-in-ag-ogue-eh'-o* translated as "bridleth" means to "curb" or to "control" ones tongue. He is saying that if we don't control what we say we deceive our own heart and our religion is vain, or useless.

This conveys a powerful concept. The implication is that what we say influences our "heart" or our attitudes. We usually think of it being the other way around.

But Jesus also referred to this relationship of words to attitudes.

Therefore take no thought, saying, What shall we eat? or, What shall we drink? or, Wherewithal shall we be clothed? (Matthew 6:31)

The context here is that he is cautioning against worrying. But notice he equates "taking thought" with "saying". In other words, a thought may come to our mind, but until we put it into words, we do not actually take ownership of it. So, he is saying that what we say is very important.

James goes on to say regarding the tongue,

For in many things we offend all. If any man offend not in word, the same is a perfect man, and able also to bridle the whole body.

Behold, we put bits in the horses' mouths, that they may obey us; and we turn about their whole body.

Behold also the ships, which though they be so great, and are driven of fierce winds, yet are they turned about with a very small helm, whithersoever the governor listeth.

Even so the tongue is a little member, and boasteth great things. Behold, how great a matter a little fire kindleth!

And the tongue is a fire, a world of iniquity; so is the tongue among our members, that it defileth the whole body, and setteth on fire the course of nature; and it is set on fire of hell.

For every kind of beasts, and of birds, and of serpents, and of things in the sea, is tamed, and hath been tamed of mankind:

But the tongue can no man tame; it is an unruly evil, full of deadly poison. (James 3:2-8)

We would do well to just meditate on these verses for a while until we grasp the power that our words have to impact our lives.

Let's just recapitulate here. First of all he says a person who doesn't offend anyone with their words is a "perfect" man and able to control the whole body. The Greek word *tel'-i-os* translated "perfect", could more accurately be translated "mature in integrity or character". I think the implication is obvious. A person who cannot control what they say cannot control their actions. As a man's tongue goes, so his whole body goes.

But the really bad news is this. "But the tongue <u>can no man tame.</u>" He is saying no man can control what they say. Well, what do we do? We submit our tongue to the Holy Spirit and let Him direct what we say. And that is why receiving our prayer language is so important. When we pray in an unknown tongue [our prayer language] the Holy Spirit "gives utterance" or gives us the words to say so that we are praying His words and not our own.

James uses the example of a ship's rudder. The smallest of parts, but as the rudder goes the whole ship goes. And he says similarly the tongue controls the way our body, and ultimately our life, goes. It logically follows that until we have submitted our tongue to the Holy Spirit, we have not totally submitted ourselves to Him.

King Solomon put it this way,

Death and life are in the power of the tongue…
(Proverbs 18:21)

This is a very powerful statement. Jesus made another powerful admonition,

But I say unto you, That every idle word that men shall speak, they shall give account thereof in the day of judgment.

For by thy words thou shalt be justified, and by thy words thou shalt be condemned.
(Matthew 12:36,37)

He says we will have to give account of every idle word. That by our words we will be justified or condemned. Why is that? Words are containers. The words we speak contain either blessing or cursing. Recall we found earlier that what we say is what we get. What we are living in today is the result of what we said yesterday. We have been given control of our own destiny and the way we exercise that control is by what we say.

If what we say has such power to affect our lives it is in our best interest to learn to control what we say. But if as James says we cannot control what we say, then what can we do? We can submit our tongues to the Holy Spirit by receiving the baptism of the Holy Spirit and allow Him to "tame" our tongue.

We are exhorted in the epistle of Jude,

But ye, beloved, building up yourselves on your most holy faith, praying in the Holy Ghost Keep yourselves in the love of God, (Jude 1:20,21)

We see that praying in the Holy Ghost (or Holy Spirit) not only builds our faith, but also keeps us in the love of God.

The apostle Paul makes it plain in this passage that praying "in the spirit" is praying in tongues.

For if I pray in an unknown tongue, my spirit prayeth, but my understanding is unfruitful.
What is it then? I will pray with the spirit, and I will pray with the understanding also
(I Corinthians 14:14,15)

He further explains,

He that speaketh in an unknown tongue edifieth himself. (I Corinthians 14:4)

The Greek word *oy-kod-om-eh'-o* translated here as "edifieth" or "edifies" can be translated as "to erect an edifice or dwelling"

When we consider this passage:

Know ye not that ye are the temple of God, and that the Spirit of God dwelleth in you?
(1 Corinthians 3:16)

As you pray in your prayer language you are making yourself a dwelling place for the Holy Spirit to live on the inside of you. In effect, the more you pray in your prayer language, the more power is imparted to your prayers.

Let's look at this again.

He that speaketh in an unknown tongue edifieth himself. (I Corinthians 14:4)

The Greek word *oy-kod-om-eh'-o* translated here as "edifieth" can also be translated as "instructs".

I really got excited when I saw this the first time. What this means is that when we pray in an "unknown" tongue, the Holy Spirit, who is giving us the words to say, is also "instructing" us. This is not surprising when Jesus has told us,

Howbeit when he, the Spirit of truth, is come, he will guide you into all truth. (John 16:13)

All truth!

And John has said,

But the anointing which ye have received of him abideth in you, and ye need not that any man teach you: but as the same anointing teacheth you of all things, and is truth, and is no lie, and even as it hath taught you, ye shall abide in him. (I John 2:27)

What both of these passages are telling us is that the Holy Spirit is sent to "instruct" us. Praying in our prayer languages is one of the means He has given us to avail ourselves of this instruction. As you spend time praying in your prayer language, for some time it may seem like nothing is really happening. You may get bored and distracted and wonder if God is really involved in the whole thing. But if you persevere, eventually you will feel flooded with revelation that would take hours to tell or write. Suddenly things you have been concerned about become totally clear and you have the complete confidence that God is taking care of it all. There will usually come to mind a scripture passage that confirms what you are receiving. If you have been praying for guidance concerning a decision you are to make the direction becomes clear. And above all, you are filled with the peace of Christ which "surpasses all understanding". (Philippians 4:7)

Another reason the apostle Paul gives us for praying in the Spirit is,

Likewise the Spirit also helpeth our infirmities: for we know not what we should pray for as we ought: but the Spirit itself maketh intercession for us with groanings which cannot be uttered. (Romans 8:26)

We see that we don't always know how to pray, or what to pray for, but the Holy Spirit makes intercession for us with "groanings which cannot be uttered". The Greek word *al-al'-ay-tos* translated here as "cannot be uttered," means "unspeakable" or "inexpressible". In other words, they are things that our natural speech is too limited to express, so they can only be expressed in a heavenly language. This is one of the reasons we need to receive it.

He goes on to say,

And he that searcheth the hearts knoweth what is the mind of the Spirit, because he maketh intercession for the saints according to the will of God. (Romans 8:27)

Again, He is saying that the Holy Spirit makes intercession for the saints [according to Bible language, this means all believers] according to the will of God. So, when we pray in our prayer language the Holy Ghost gives us the words to say to direct our prayers according to His wisdom.

Suppose I said to you that I know someone who desires to be your prayer partner. This person is available anytime, night or day. It is a person who knows you better than you know yourself and knows exactly how to pray in a way that is best for you. And best of all, this person's prayers are ALWAYS answered. Are you interested? Then let me introduce you. Just say "Hello, Holy Spirit".

Begin today to set aside a specific time to "Present your body as a living sacrifice, holy and acceptable to God" (Romans 12:1) [preferably first thing in the morning] and allow the Holy Spirit to use your tongue to pray out His perfect plan for your life. Begin by even 15 minutes a day and watch what happens. Soon it will not be a matter of effort to start, it will be something you do not want to stop.

If you have been born again, and would like to receive the baptism in the Holy Spirit, pray this prayer

Heavenly Father, I thank you that I have been born again by the blood of Jesus and counted worthy to receive Him into my life. Please baptize me in your Holy Spirit and enable me to pray in a Heavenly language so that I can yield my tongue to you and pray out your plans for my life and for those for whom you call me to intercede. I want to be totally yielded to you so that in all things in every area of my life your will shall be done. I thank you that you are faithful to do it. That when I ask for the Holy Spirit I will receive Him and nothing else because I ask this through Christ my Lord. AMEN

If you have prayed this prayer, God is faithful who has promised and He will do what He has said He will do. He has promised that whoever asks for the Holy Spirit will receive Him so it is already done. Begin to thank Him and whatever words come to your mouth to say, speak them forth. They may sound funny and strange because it will be a language you don't know. But God is faithful and you can be sure that the words you speak are words that the Holy Spirit has given you to say. Spend some time just worshipping Him and thanking Him for the precious gift of Himself.

Speak the Word

*But the righteousness which is of faith **speaketh** on this wise...But what **saith** it? The word is nigh thee, [even] in thy mouth, and in thy heart: that is, the word of faith, which we preach;*

*That if thou shalt **confess with thy mouth** the Lord Jesus, and shalt believe in thine heart that God hath raised him from the dead, thou shalt be saved.* (Romans 10:6, 8, 9)

We are told:

"As ye have therefore received Christ Jesus the Lord, [so] walk ye in him:" (Colossians 2:6)

How do we do this? Well how did we receive Him? Look at the scripture here from Romans. It tells us we received Him by believing in our heart and confessing with our mouth the "Word of faith" concerning Him, which was that God has raised Him from the dead.

We see here a spiritual principal. When we not only believe the Word in our heart, but confess it with our mouth, we shall see it performed in our lives.

But you say, you have already done that and you haven't seen any result

We need to check, then what *else* we are "confessing". The Greek word *"homologeo"* translated here as "confess" means literally "to say the same thing". We need to be continually "saying the same thing" as the Word.

We are told in James that we are to ask in faith "nothing wavering". (James 1:6) In other words, what are we saying the rest of the time. Are our words lining up with our faith, are we continually confessing our confidence in the Word which says:

Whatsoever you ask the Father in my name He will do. (John 14:13)

or are we believing and saying what we see and feel according to our circumstances.

Put another way, Jesus said:

For verily I say unto you, That whosoever shall say unto this mountain, Be thou removed, and be thou cast into the sea; and <u>shall not doubt in his</u>

heart, but shall believe that those things which he saith shall come to pass; he shall have whatsoever he saith. (Mark 11:23)

So we see that faith is a *decision.* We must refuse to doubt, once we have begun in prayer, and we must continue to believe that the things we have said in prayer shall come to pass, and we will have what we **say.** It is significant that He uses the word "say" three times here, while He uses the word "believe" only once.

There is great power in our words, and until we realize this and take custody of our words, speaking only those things which are in agreement with the Word of God, we will never see the power in our prayers which God intended us to have.

God created the world by Words. We read in Genesis that he said "Let there be light and there was light". (Gen 1:3) Reading on we see that this is how he continued to create. He simply spoke it, and it was, just as He said. He continues to maintain the universe by the power of His Word. (Hebrews 1:3)

The Bible then goes on to say that God said:

Let us create man in our image. (Gen 1:26)

What does this mean? Well, it means just what it says. He created us to be just like Himself. If

God spoke and it was, then when we speak it is. We get what we say! What we are walking in today is a product of what we said yesterday. If we want to change our circumstances, we must change what we are saying.

You think this sounds pretty presumptuous? Well, let us compare scripture with scripture and see if we find anything else to support it.

We are told by the apostle John:

...as He is, so are we in this world. (I John 4:17)

He was referring to Jesus here. And how was Jesus? Well, He said Himself,

...he that hath seen me hath seen the Father. (John 14:9)

So we see Jesus is just like the Father. So if we are to be like Jesus, and Jesus is just like the Father, it follows we are to be like the Father.

Consider this passage:

Be ye therefore followers of God, as dear children; And it was Jesus who told us: (Ephesians 5:1)

The Greek word *mimētēs* translated as "followers" is more accurately translated as "imitators". So we are told to be imitators of God. In other words, we are to act like God does. And the way God is to create by speaking. God said "Light be", and light was. (Genesis 1:3) acts

Notice what Jesus said:

For verily I say unto you, That whosoever shall **say** *unto this mountain, Be thou removed, and be thou cast into the sea; and shall not doubt in his heart, but shall believe that those things which he* **saith** *shall come to pass; he shall have whatsoever he* **saith**. (Mark 1:23)

Jesus was very concerned with our words and having us be good stewards of the power that they contain. He tells us further;

But I say unto you, That **every idle word** *that men shall speak, they shall give account thereof in the day of judgment.* (Matt 12:26)

Similarly, James warns us:

If any man among you seem to be religious, and bridleth not his tongue, but deceiveth his own heart, this man's religion [is] vain. (James 1:26)

We need to constantly become aware of what we are saying and refuse to speak things which are contrary to God's Word, as we can be confident that God's Word is His express will in our lives.

Meditate on God's Word:

Notice we are told that the Word of God is given for our benefit.

All scripture is given by inspiration of God, and is profitable for doctrine, for reproof, for correction, for instruction in righteousness:

That the man of God may be perfect, throughly furnished unto all good works.
(2 Timothy 3:16, 17)

Further, we know that all the promises in God are "yes and amen" for us.

For all the promises of God in him are yea, and in him Amen, unto the glory of God by us.
(2 Corinthians 1:20)

This book of the law shall not depart out of thy mouth; but thou shalt meditate therein day and night, that thou mayest observe to do according to all that is written therein: for then thou shalt make thy way prosperous, and then thou shalt have good success. (Joshua 1:8)

Notice "this book of the law" or God's Word, shall not "depart out your mouth". But we are to "meditate" on it continually. The Hebrew word translated as "meditate" means "to mutter softly". So we need to continually speak the Word to ourselves.

We appropriate the promises of God by personalizing them and speaking them into our lives.

We having the same spirit of faith, according as it is written, I believed, and therefore have I spoken; we also believe, and therefore speak; (2 Corinthians 4:13)

Notice Jesus said:

Have faith in God.
For verily I say unto you, That whosoever shall say unto this mountain, Be thou removed, and be thou cast into the sea; and shall not doubt in his heart, but shall believe that those things which he saith shall come to pass; he shall have whatsoever he saith. (Mark 11:23)

He is saying here that whoever <u>says</u> to the mountain "Be cast into the sea" and does not doubt in his heart, but believes the thing he <u>says</u> will come to past, will have whatever he <u>says</u>.

126

Notice he uses the word "says" here three times, and He only uses the word "believes" one time. Speaking the Word activates faith.

Jesus then goes on to say :

Therefore I say unto you, What things soever ye desire, when ye pray, believe that ye receive them, and ye shall have them. (Mar 11:24)

Notice we are to believe we receive **when we pray**! Not when we see the results.

When I first got hold of these concepts I was having chronic sinus infections which were no longer responding to any antibiotic. So I said "Father God, your Word says Jesus bore my sickness and my diseases and by His stripes I am healed, so I command these sinuses to drain and heal according to the Word of God that says I am healed" and I continued to thank God for healing me for three days until the symptoms left.

This is why I am, at age 70, still healthy and working and have no "diseases of aging" and people usually assume I am about 50. I claim, almost every day, "My youth is renewed like the eagle" (Psalm 103:5)

Remember;

No Word of God is without power (Luke 1:37)

Then said the LORD unto me, Thou hast well seen: for I will hasten [watch over] *my word to perform it.* (Jeremiah 1:12)

So shall my word be that goeth forth out of my mouth: it shall not return unto me void, but it shall accomplish that which I please, and it shall prosper in the thing whereto I sent it.
(Isaiah 55:11)

No Word of God is without power. He watches over His Word to perform it and His Word will not return to Him void but it will accomplish what He sent it to us to do.

Scriptures for meditation
to build faith:

As you meditate on these Scriptures, make them
personal. For example:

When we read:

*Himself took our infirmities, and bare our
sicknesses.* (Matthew 8:17)

...by whose stripes ye were healed.
(1 Peter 2:24)

we say "Jesus, I thank you that You bore my
sickness and my infirmities, and now Father I
receive the healing that Jesus already purchased
for me. I will thank you and praise you from this
moment on that Jesus bore my sickness and my
diseases and by His stripes I am healed by the
Blood of Jesus, in Jesus' Name."

Then whenever you think of it, or a symptom
persists, you continue to say "Father I just thank
you and praise you that your word is truth. Jesus
promised that whatever I asked in His Name He

would do, I asked according to Your Word, in Jesus Name, therefore it is done and I am healed."

Do the same for any other promise contained in the Word.

Again, we can say "Father, you said you are not willing that any should parish. You said you have given us a new covenant that you would write your laws on our hearts. Jesus said "Whoever sins you remit are remitted and whoever sins you retain are retained", so I pray for ___ that you forgive their sins and write your law on their heart. I ask that you give them a hunger for holiness, righteousness and truth. That you lead them in paths of righteousness for your name sake (Psalm 23) and I thank you that you are faithful and you are working your will in their lives to set them free and bring them to Christ"

Healing:

And ye shall serve the LORD your God, and he shall bless thy bread, and thy water; and I will take sickness away from the midst of thee. (Exodus 23:25)

for I am the LORD that healeth thee. (Exodus 15:26)

Bless the LORD, O my soul: and all that is within me, bless his holy name.
Bless the LORD, O my soul, and forget not all his benefits:
... who healeth all thy diseases;
Who satisfieth thy mouth with good things; so that thy youth is renewed like the eagle's.
(Psalm 103: 2,3,5)

Himself took our infirmities, and bare our sicknesses.
by whose stripes ye were healed.
(Matthew 8:17, 1 Peter 2:24)

My son, attend to my words; incline thine ear unto my sayings.
Let them not depart from thine eyes; keep them in the midst of thine heart.
For they are life unto those that find them, and health to all their flesh. (Proverbs 4:20 - 22)

Anti-aging:

Bless the LORD, O my soul, and forget not all his benefits:
...who healeth all thy diseases;
...Who satisfieth thy mouth with good things; so that thy youth is renewed like the eagle's.
(Psalm 103: 2,3,5)

His flesh shall be fresher than a child's: he shall return to the days of his youth: (Job 33:25)

131

And Moses was an hundred and twenty years old when he died: his eye was not dim, nor his natural force abated. (Deuteronomy 34:7)

And the LORD said, My spirit shall not always strive with man, for that he also is flesh: yet his days shall be an hundred and twenty years (Genesis 6:3)

Because he hath set his love upon me, therefore will I deliver him: I will set him on high, because he hath known my name.
He shall call upon me, and I will answer him: I will be with him in trouble; I will deliver him, and honour him.
With <u>long life</u> will I satisfy him, and shew him my salvation. (Psalm 91:14 - 16)

My son, forget not my law; but let thine heart keep my commandments:
For length of days, and <u>long life</u>, and peace, shall they add to thee. (Proverbs 3:1,2)

For who hath known the mind of the Lord, that he may instruct him? But we have the mind of Christ. (1Corinthians 2:16)

Financial prosperity:

But thou shalt remember the LORD thy God: for it is he that giveth thee power to get wealth, that he may establish his covenant which he sware unto thy fathers, as it is this day.
(Deuteronomy 8:18)

The blessing of the LORD, it maketh rich, and he addeth no sorrow with it. (Proverbs 10:22)

For ye know the grace of our Lord Jesus Christ, that, though he was rich, yet for your sakes he became poor, that ye through his poverty might be rich.(2 Corinthians 8:9)

And God is able to make all grace abound toward you; that ye, always having all sufficiency in all things, may abound to every good work:

(As it is written, He hath dispersed abroad; he hath given to the poor: his righteousness remaineth for ever.

Now he that ministereth seed to the sower both minister bread for your food, and multiply your seed sown, and increase the fruits of your righteousness;)

Being enriched in every thing to all bountifulness, which causeth through us thanksgiving to God. (2 Corinthians 9:8 - 11)

Honour the LORD with thy substance, and with the firstfruits of all thine increase:

So shall thy barns be filled with plenty, and thy presses shall burst out with new wine.
(Proverbs 3:9, 10)

But my God shall supply all your need according to his riches in glory by Christ Jesus. (Philippians 4:19)

Bring ye all the tithes into the storehouse, that there may be meat in mine house, and prove me now herewith, saith the LORD of hosts, if I will not open you the windows of heaven, and pour you out a blessing, that there shall not be room enough to receive it.

And I will rebuke the devourer for your sakes, and he shall not destroy the fruits of your ground; neither shall your vine cast her fruit before the time in the field, saith the LORD of hosts. (Malachi 3:10, 11)

And all these blessings shall come on thee, and overtake thee, if thou shalt hearken unto the voice of the LORD thy God.

Blessed shall be thy basket and thy store.

The LORD shall command the blessing upon thee in thy storehouses, and in all that thou settest thine hand unto; and he shall bless thee in the land which the LORD thy God giveth thee.

And the LORD shall make thee plenteous in goods, in the fruit of thy body, and in the fruit of thy cattle, and in the fruit of thy ground, in the land which the LORD sware unto thy fathers to give thee. (Deuteronomy 28:2, 5, 8, 11)

Children:

And all thy children shall be taught of the LORD; and great shall be the peace of thy children. (Isaiah 54:13)

But thus saith the LORD, Even the captives of the mighty shall be taken away, and the prey of the terrible shall be delivered: for I will contend with him that contendeth with thee, and I will save thy children. (Isaiah 49:25)

Though hand join in hand, the wicked shall not be unpunished: but the seed of the righteous shall be delivered. (Proverbs 11:21)

For I will pour water upon him that is thirsty, and floods upon the dry ground: I will pour my spirit upon thy seed, and my blessing upon thine offspring: (Isaiah 44:3)

As for me, this is my covenant with them, saith the LORD; My spirit that is upon thee, and my words which I have put in thy mouth, shall not depart out of thy mouth, nor out of the mouth of thy seed, nor out of the mouth of thy seed's seed, saith the LORD, from henceforth and for ever. (Isaiah 59:21)

Stress/Anxiety/Fear/Worry:

- Please note, stress, anxiety and worry are all just manifestations of fear.

For God hath not given us the spirit of fear; but of power, and of love, and of a sound mind.
(2 Timothy 1:7)

Behold, I give unto you power to tread on serpents and scorpions, and over all the power of the enemy: and nothing shall by any means hurt you (Luke 10:19)

Submit yourselves therefore to God. Resist the devil, and he will flee from you. (James 4:7)

Be careful [anxious] *for nothing; but in every thing by prayer and supplication with thanksgiving let your requests be made known unto God.* (Philippians 4:6)

Be strong and of a good courage, fear not, nor be afraid of them: for the LORD thy God, he it is that doth go with thee; he will not fail thee, nor forsake thee. (Deuteronomy 31:6)
Let not your heart be troubled: ye believe in God, believe also in me. (John 14:1)

Peace I leave with you, my peace I give unto you: not as the world giveth, give I unto you. Let not your heart be troubled, neither let it be afraid. (John 14:27)

Many are the afflictions of the righteous: but the LORD delivereth him out of them all.
(Psalm 34:19)

These things I have spoken unto you, that in me ye might have peace. In the world ye shall have tribulation: but be of good cheer; I have overcome the world
(John 16:33)

...fear not, for I am with thee (Genesis 26:24)

...as I was with Moses, so I will be with thee: I will not fail thee, nor forsake thee. (Joshua 1:5)

And they overcame him by the blood of the Lamb, and by the word of their testimony;
(Revelation 12:11)

Wisdom:

If any of you lack wisdom, let him ask of God, that giveth to all men liberally, and upbraideth not; and it shall be given him. (James 1:5)

But of him [God] *are ye in Christ Jesus, who of God is made unto us wisdom, and righteousness, and sanctification, and redemption:*
(1 Corinthians 1:30)

My son, forget not my law; but let thine heart keep my commandments:
For length of days, and long life, and peace, shall they add to thee.

Let not mercy and truth forsake thee: bind them about thy neck; write them upon the table of thine heart:
So shalt thou find favour and good understanding in the sight of God and man.
Trust in the LORD with all thine heart; and lean not unto thine own understanding.
In all thy ways acknowledge him, and he shall direct thy paths.
Be not wise in thine own eyes: fear the LORD, and depart from evil.
It shall be health to thy navel, and marrow to thy bones. (Proverbs 3:1- 8)

My son, despise not the chastening of the LORD; neither be weary of his correction:
For whom the LORD loveth he correcteth; even as a father the son in whom he delighteth.
Happy is the man that findeth wisdom, and the man that getteth understanding.
For the merchandise of it is better than the merchandise of silver, and the gain thereof than fine gold.
She is more precious than rubies: and all the things thou canst desire are not to be compared unto her.
Length of days is in her right hand; and in her left hand riches and honour.
Her ways are ways of pleasantness, and all her paths are peace.
She is a tree of life to them that lay hold upon her: and happy is every one that retaineth her.
The LORD by wisdom hath founded the earth; by

By his knowledge the depths are broken up, and the clouds drop down the dew.

My son, let not them depart from thine eyes: keep sound wisdom and discretion:

So shall they be life unto thy soul, and grace to thy neck.

Then shalt thou walk in thy way safely, and thy foot shall not stumble.

When thou liest down, thou shalt not be afraid: yea, thou shalt lie down, and thy sleep shall be sweet.

Be not afraid of sudden fear, neither of the desolation of the wicked, when it cometh.

For the LORD shall be thy confidence, and shall keep thy foot from being taken. (Pro 3:11 - 26)

Salvation for others:

My little children, of whom I travail in birth again until Christ be formed in you,
(Galations 4:19)

The Lord is not slack concerning his promise, as some men count slackness; but is longsuffering to us-ward, not willing that any should perish, but that all should come to repentance.
(2 Peter 3:9)

Finally, my brethren, be strong in the Lord, and in the power of his might.

Put on the whole armour of God, that ye may be able to stand against the wiles of the devil.
(Ephesians 6:12)

For we wrestle not against flesh and blood, but against principalities, against powers, against the rulers of the darkness of this world, against spiritual wickedness in high places.
(Ephesians 6:10, 11)

For though we walk in the flesh, we do not war after the flesh:

(For the weapons of our warfare are not carnal, but mighty through God to the pulling down of strong holds;)

For it is God which worketh in you both to will and to do of his good pleasure.
(Philippians 2:13)

He restoreth my soul: he leadeth me in the paths of righteousness for his name's sake.
(Psalms 23:3)

Casting down imaginations, and every high thing that exalteth itself against the knowledge of God, and bringing into captivity every thought to the obedience of Christ; (Colossians 10:3 - 5)

Then will I sprinkle clean water upon you, and ye shall be clean: from all your filthiness, and from all your idols, will I cleanse you.

A new heart also will I give you, and a new spirit will I put within you: and I will take away the stony heart out of your flesh, and I will give you an heart of flesh. (Ezekiel 36:25, 26)

And I will put my spirit within you, and cause you to walk in my statutes, and ye shall keep my judgments, and do them.

And ye shall dwell in the land that I gave to your fathers; and ye shall be my people, and I will be your God.

I will also save you from all your uncleannesses: and I will call for the corn, and will increase it, and lay no famine upon you.

And I will multiply the fruit of the tree, and the increase of the field, that ye shall receive no more reproach of famine among the heathen.

Then shall ye remember your own evil ways, and your doings that were not good, and shall lothe yourselves in your own sight for your iniquities and for your abominations. (Ezekiel 36:27, 31)

This is the covenant that I will make with them after those days, saith the Lord, I will put my laws into their hearts, and in their minds will I write them;

And their sins and iniquities will I remember no more. (Hebrews 10:16, 17)

Behold, I will gather them out of all countries, whither I have driven them in mine anger, and in my fury, and in great wrath; and I will bring them again unto this place, and I will cause them to dwell safely:

And they shall be my people, and I will be their God:

And I will give them one heart, and one way, that they may fear me for ever, for the good of them, and of their children after them:

And I will make an everlasting covenant with them, that I will not turn away from them, to do them good; but I will put my fear in their hearts, that they shall not depart from me.
(Jeremiah 32:37 - 40)

In Conclusion:

Hopefully, by now, you are getting the picture. Your destiny is in your heart and in your mouth.

I call heaven and earth to record this day against you, that I have set before you life and death, blessing and cursing: therefore choose life, that both thou and thy seed may live: (Deuteronomy 30:19)

Death and life are in the power of the tongue: and they that love it shall eat the fruit thereof. (Proverbs 18:21)

Build your faith by feeding on the Word every day and pray this prayer each day:

Let the words of my mouth, and the meditation of my heart, be acceptable in thy sight, O LORD, my strength, and my redeemer. (Psalms 19:14)

Then watch as God's Word begins to transform your life into "days of Heaven on the earth".

Therefore shall ye lay up these my words in your heart and in your soul, and bind them for a sign upon your hand, that they may be as frontlets between your eyes.

And ye shall teach them your children, speaking of them when thou sittest in thine house, and when thou walkest by the way, when thou liest down, and when thou risest up.

And thou shalt write them upon the door posts of thine house, and upon thy gates:

That your days may be multiplied, and the days of your children, in the land which the LORD sware unto your fathers to give them, as the days of heaven upon the earth.
(Deuteronomy 11:18 - 21)

Made in the USA
Middletown, DE
08 February 2016